Catching Up

Catching Up

The official history of the Eastern Illinois Baseball League

by Fred Kroner

Published by The News-Gazette

The News-Gazette®

EDITOR AND PUBLISHER	John Foreman
EXECUTIVE EDITOR	John Beck
MANAGING EDITOR	Dan Corkery
SPORTS EDITOR	Jim Rossow
PHOTO EDITOR	Darrell Hoemann
PROJECT MANAGER	Amy George

Front cover photo: Darrell Hoemann, The News-Gazette
Cover design and book layout: Joan Millis, The News-Gazette

ISBN: 978-0-09846063-0-6

© 2010 by The News-Gazette, Inc.

Printed in the United States of America

The News-Gazette, Inc.
15 Main Street
Champaign, IL 61820
Phone: (217) 351-5252
Fax: (217) 351-5245
www.news-gazette.com

Dedication

For my wife, Emily Kroner, the best sport I know

Special thanks and credits

*To Carol and Louie Krumwiede for their fact-checking and research,
and for providing pictures and other memorabilia;
To The News-Gazette for the use of its archives and file photos;
To Amy George, Joan Millis and Mike Goebel, from The News-Gazette,
for their outstanding efforts in the production, editing,
layout and organization of the book.*

Contents

In the beginning

Before air conditioning or ESPN, there was the Eastern Illinois Baseball League. Before heart transplants or AIDS, there was the Eastern Illinois Baseball League. Before man walked on the moon or fought a second World War, there was the Eastern Illinois Baseball League.

It has continued to thrive and survive as the world has advanced to an age where communication is done via text messages, and virtual games, which don't require physical strength or dexterity, have become staples of the society.

The 2010 summer season marks the "official" 75th anniversary of the E.I. Baseball League. That's a decade more than when the Chicago Cubs last played in a World Series and eight years longer than the lifespan of the first President of the United States.

The E.I. Baseball League is an organization for amateur ball players who are annually attracted to the summer playgrounds, their hometowns ranging from Kankakee to Robinson and from Danville to Lexington.

Jeff Demith played for 18 summers in the E.I., all with Thomasboro, and established the record for career hits.

"It wasn't just a baseball team," Demith said. "It was an extended family. These were the people you socialized with all year. We celebrated weddings, births and, unfortunately, deaths of close ones.

"E.I. baseball was not just a game. It was a way of life. It was what you did from Mother's Day until Labor Day. It was what you looked forward to all winter.

"To this day, I consider them the best friends of my life. Even though we don't see each other as much as we'd like, we still share the memories of some of the best times of our lives and it is something I will cherish until the day I die."

Only one community — Buckley — has fielded a team all 75 years of the E.I.'s existence, but at one time or another, 51 communities have proudly claimed to be the home of an E.I. team.

An original Buckley Dutch Master, Earl Gehle recounted in a 1976 *News-*

Members of the Buckley Dutch Masters' 1936 team, which participated in the first year of the Eastern Illinois Baseball League. In front, from left, are: Orval Klann, Tom Hull, Earl Gehle and Reinold Wolf. In the middle row, from left, are: Charlie Klann, Mark Kaufmann, Jack Wilkens, Arno Krumwiede, Walt Krumwiede and Arlie Seymour. In back, from left, are Carl Ecker, Ed Knueppel, unknown, Dickie Janssen and Harry Strauss.

Gazette article who he considered the top batsman from the early years.

"Dill Seymour was the toughest out," Gehle said. "He could hit a walnut with a broomstick."

Among the E.I. alumni are athletes who have played in the major leagues (including Darrin Fletcher, Tom Fletcher, Scott Garrelts, Matt Herges, Dick Hyde, Walt Linden, Marty Pattin, Kevin Seitzer and Sterling Slaughter), an athlete who went on to become a major league umpire (Mark Carlson) and another who played briefly in the majors but eventually became a major league manager (John Felske).

Carlson played for Tolono from 1988-1990. By 1999, he was a major league umpire. In 2003 he worked the All-Star Game, and in 2007 he was assigned to the N.L. Division Series.

Felske, an athlete at the University of Illinois, was a catcher who played for Royal in 1960.

"What's ironic," Tom Fletcher said, "is that he was our No. 2 catcher. He was behind Leon Busboom."

Felske played 54 games (four with the Chicago Cubs in 1968) in the major leagues and went on to manage the Philadelphia Phillies from Sept. 30, 1984 to June 18, 1987, compiling a career record of 190-194.

A year after he played for Royal — in August 1961 — Felske was signed as a free agent by the Cubs.

Herges was the E.I. Player of the Week on Sept. 2, 1990, the week following a no-hitter that he pitched for Gifford-Flatville.

Linden was the catcher and cleanup hitter for Flatville when it opened the 1953 season against a Monticello team managed by Ecus Vaughn and Loren Tate. The 29-year-old Linden, who had played for the Illini, played three games in the majors for the 1950 Boston Braves.

Not everyone associated with E.I. who achieved future fame played the game. The 1948 E.I. Tournament championship game was covered for the *Champaign-Urbana Courier* by a person who went on to became a nationally acclaimed critic, Gene Shalit.

His lead in the Aug. 30, 1948 editions from a game played in Royal: "Royal's baseball team, as scorned as a pound of margarine in Wisconsin, overcame intense heat and two heavy leads here Sunday to win the Eastern Illinois Tournament, much to the surprise of everyone, including themselves."

Down 6-5, the Giants used a seven-run eighth inning and went on to beat Seymour 13-6.

Besides those individuals, E.I. has been home to hundreds of other baseball players for whom the league was their major league, and they played with the heart and passion of their brethren whom we've seen on television earning millions of dollars.

There are stories of success (such as pitchers who threw every inning of a doubleheader; and a batter whose league debut resulted in an 8 for 8 performance), stories of dedication (such as the athlete who played in an E.I. game the day after his wedding) and stories that put the league on the front page of newspapers (such as the time Satchel Paige and the touring Kansas City Monarchs were beaten in an exhibition game against E.I. All-Stars; and the time Dizzy Dean pitched five innings for Flatville).

"It was Americana at its best, a Sunday afternoon spent at the ballpark," said left-hander Kevin Sprau, who holds the all-time record for pitching victories (125).

There was perhaps not a more memorable — or smashing — debut than that of 22-year-old left-handed hitting Cliff McIntosh, the third first baseman employed by Gifford-Flatville in the 1988 season. The former Southern Illinois University athlete arrived for a June 12 doubleheader at Tolono and by day's end was 8 for 8 with four home runs (two in each game) and 15 runs batted in.

Appropriately, he had been installed as the Giflats' cleanup hitter. G-F split the twin bill, losing 14-10 before winning 15-5. McIntosh showed his play was no fluke a week later. He was walked on four of his eight at-bats but went 3 for 4 against Thomasboro with a home run and four RBI in another Gifford-Flatville split.

The desire to not miss a game is so strong for some that they plan their wedding around an open week in the schedule.

T.J. Posey and Stacey Perkinson were married on July 28, 2001.

"Trent Eshleman (Buckley manager) made sure at the preseason meeting that Buckley had a bye the weekend of our wedding," T.J. Posey said.

Two years earlier, Brian Naese was not quite as fortunate with the timing of his marriage to the former Laurie Haag. They were wed the day before the 1999 tournament championship game in Buckley.

"It was, and always will be, understood in Buckley that nothing gets in the way of the E.I. Tourney championship," said Eshleman, who was the best man at Naese's wedding. Sure enough, Naese was in his customary position of left field when the title game began.

Buckley won the game against Paxton, scoring three runs in the bottom of the 10th. Eshleman had the walkoff, game-winning hit, but said, "that is not what makes the game most memorable.

"The most memorable part was the limousine that pulled up to escort Brian Naese and his wife to the O'Hare airport for their honeymoon. Although the game was not over, Naese did have to succumb to his new bride and leave the dugout, board the limo and take off to catch their flight. The Dutch Master crowd applauded."

The diamond at Buckley took on a special meaning for another former Dutch Master.

"My best friend, Steve Ekhoff, proposed to his wife on the mound at Scheiwe Field," Posey said.

Many premier E.I. players were courted by coaches in other leagues, especially ones in suburban Chicago. Eshleman remained loyal to E.I.

"My simple reply to them was, 'You can't begin to give me, nor understand, what the E.I. League gives to me. We have fans, lots of them, at every game and they make the E.I. League a much better atmosphere to learn about pressure and hone baseball skills than playing games against more teams in front of a handful of player's wives, girlfriends and parents.'"

A view of the Buckley Dutch Masters' home field, looking in from right field, in 1983.

Virgil Scheiwe

E.I. has developed into a close-knit fraternity, but one which includes more than the athletes.

"Our wives have become friends, our children have grown up together and they would all say it has been worth it," Eshleman said. "Anyone in the Dutch Master family would do anything for each other. We have helped each other out in a multitude of ways and have done so at the drop of a hat with a quick phone call. Players and fans have bought each other many drinks, but have gone far beyond that, helping each other get jobs, pay debts, find shelter when things weren't going well, and countless other examples."

There are families (such as the Fletchers, Franzens, Loschens and Scheiwes) whose associations with the league surpasses seven decades.

Buckley's field was named after Virgil Scheiwe on May 30, 1999. His name is displayed in 12-inch block letters on the scoreboard, located in center field, 415 feet from home plate. Scheiwe's legend extended beyond his pitching (which started for the team in 1942), coaching and groundskeeping exploits.

"Virgil was a great soothsayer who would offer valuable advice to those playing and managing, and instill in those around the organization the fundamentals of the game and to life," Eshleman said. "I recall him personally telling me after I hit an Opening Day home run in Gifford that he 'hated to see little guys like me hit home runs because then we would think we could always hit them.' I recall taking heed to that advice about swinging for the fences, especially after going 0-for-the-next-3 weeks.

"The man, the rock of the Buckley Dutch Masters even to this day in spirit alone is undoubtedly Virgil Scheiwe."

After Scheiwe's death on Sept. 9, 2006, at age 82, Pastor Mark Haller from St. John's Lutheran Church in Buckley, made reference to the baseball connections in his eulogy.

"He mentioned this Dutch Master 'family' and Virgil's commitment to it, and its place in the 'game of life,' for those connected to it," Eshleman said.

The list of E.I. alums includes one of the most storied coaches in University of Illinois history. During his heyday as a player, Harry Combes was an E.I. batting champion.

There have been controversies as well as championships. Something supposedly as simple as when the league originated is shrouded in doubt. Documents show that three men organized an amateur baseball league on March 31, 1933. The trio was Jack Waldron, an Urbana woodworker, Elvin 'Dock' Leedy, an Ogden restaurateur, and Shelby Himes, the owner of a Champaign sporting goods store.

However, it was not until 1936 that the league took on the name, Eastern Illinois Baseball League, which makes the 2010 season the "official" 75th anniversary season.

Prior to being known as the Eastern Illinois Baseball League, the organization was named for its location: the Champaign County League. When Buckley, which first started playing ball in the late 1920s, petitioned for entry in 1935 followed by Rankin in 1936, the moniker of Eastern Central Illinois Baseball League was eventually adopted.

Jack Waldron, the first E.I. League President

However, it was considered unwieldy and former *News-Gazette* sports writer E.W. Hesse wrote on July 11, 1982: "By midsummer (1936), headline writers and fans alike began referring to the circuit simply as the E.I. League."

In a 1976 interview, Waldron told *The News-Gazette*, "I remember the first time an E.I. team had nerve enough to ask its fans to pay admission to see a game. I don't remember what they charged, but the total gate receipts were $3.65."

Buckley's long time business manager, Arlie Seymour, who spent 19 years with the organization until the early 1950s, was behind the decision to charge admission, which was set at 25 cents for adults and 15 cents for children.

In a 1953 *News-Gazette* story written by Fowler Connell, Seymour said he had attended a game in Buckley and asked where the gatekeeper was. Upon learning there was not one, Connell reported that he responded, "How do you expect to make any money unless you charge the fans to see your team?"

Seymour showed his promotional skills, scheduling events in addition to baseball to draw fans. Among his ideas were horse races, parachute jumps, a sheep dog act, gate prizes and a boxing match.

Himes, Leedy and Waldron were known as the 'Commissioners Three,' and their service was uninterrupted until Leedy died in 1951. The meeting room at Bailey & Himes Sporting Goods, in Champaign's Campustown where E.I. business was conducted, was named the Leedy Room in his honor.

Others instrumental in the original organization of the amateur league were Bert Coleman, Al Nelson and Clark Thomas.

Less than a month after the first meeting in 1933, 10 teams were playing. Those teams, and their managers, were:

Bondville, Ray Brown; Flatville, John Franzen; Gifford, Ted Siddens;

St. Mary's of Champaign, Leo Eisminger; Ogden, George Mead; Parkville, V.H. Wilson; Rantoul, Francis Walsh; Sidney, Ray Young; Tolono, manager unknown; Urbana, Bert Coleman

The first championship was won by the Urbana Merchants, who also won the postseason tournament.

One of the E.I.'s first veterans was Seymour's Arnold 'Dutch' Young, the only person to play in each of the league's first 14 years of existence. In the 10 years in which statistics were available, he batted .305 (176 for 577).

He was one of four brothers who were in the lineup for the E.I. entry, based in Seymour, joining George 'Ding' Young, Forrest 'Coonie' Young and Everett 'Babe' Young. Dutch Young spent seven of his years as a player-manager.

In 1949, Dutch Young, 38, died from polio and the Bondville Community Club sponsored the Young Memorial Trophy, which for years was presented to the E.I. batting champion. The first recipient in 1949 was Sidney's Hugh 'Bud' Bitter, who batted .468. Bitter went 3 for 4 in his final game to edge Flatville's Ralph Loschen, who went 2 for 4 and settled for a .444 runner-up average. They could each track the other's final-game progress as their teams played against one another.

All-time best

Trying to determine the top player in the history of the Eastern Illinois Baseball League is similar to selecting which penny released recently from the Denver Mint is the shiniest.

There's a roster full of ultra-deserving candidates, including Ralph Loschen, the greatest ambassador, whose association encompasses nearly 70 years, Kevin Sprau, the career wins leader who is regarded as the premier left-handed pitcher, Virgil Scheiwe, who has a field named after him (at Buckley) as well as an award (Pitcher of the Year), Jeff Demith, the all-time hits leader, Bill Elliott, who set season and career home run records and Mike Scholz, who in various newspaper accounts was referred to as "the Cy Young of the E.I. League."

Scholz ultimately rates the nod both for his personal success as well as how he helped elevate the Gifford-Flatville teams on which he played. In 10 of the first 11 years he played E.I. baseball, the Giflats won either the regular season or the tournament championship or both. He played on 14 championship teams.

In 2009, Gifford-Flatville's Mike Scholz was chosen by The News-Gazette as the E.I.'s top all-time player.

Including postseason play, Scholz amassed a 97-16 career record and registered at least 100 strikeouts in six consecutive seasons, all with Loschen and Dick Franzen as the co-coaches.

He was at his best in what has been anointed the top game played in a league that traces its history three-quarters of a century. *The News-Gazette* heading over the 1974 tournament championship game box score read, "The Greatest Title Game."

On the afternoon of Aug. 24, Scholz struck out 27 batters and allowed eight hits in a 15-inning marathon during which regular season co-champs Gifford-Flatville and Rantoul played one scoreless inning after another.

Scholz and his catcher that day, his brother Pat, each had two hits in the game, accounting for half of the eight hits the team managed against Steve Ward.

"It seemed like both guys got better as the game went on," Loschen said. Writing in *The News-Gazette*, E.W. Hesse reported the game was "... waged in perfect baseball weather before one of the largest and most appreciative crowds in E.I. history."

The Giflats prevailed 1-0 in the 15th when Dwayne Gossett scored on Phil Rogers' sacrifice fly in foul territory near the right field bullpen.

Scholz, now an assistant principal at St. Thomas More High School in Champaign, said "for days after that game, I was so sore I couldn't do anything."

The former UI athlete added "that was the best baseball game I ever participated in."

During his days as an Illini, the Decatur St. Teresa graduate pitched in the summer Central Illinois Collegiate League.

"The E.I. was not a step down from the CICL," he said. "You had to be on top of your game every Sunday."

In his youth, Scholz was used to playing with high-caliber players. One of his teammates with the Decatur American Legion team was future major league batting champion Bill Madlock.

"I loved baseball," Scholz said. "I couldn't be around it enough.

"My dad and mom built a baseball park in our backyard. My brother and I cut where the bases went and we played every day, sun up to sun down, until we couldn't see anymore."

The dominant E.I. pitcher of the 1970s, Scholz never had an E.I. season where he lost more than two games. His 12-0 record in 1976 featured his pitching in both games of a regular season-ending doubleheader sweep, which the Giflats needed to clinch the title. The performance enhanced his "Iron Mike" reputation.

"You couldn't get him out of the game," Loschen said. "I'd go to the mound and he'd say, 'Get back in the dugout.' He's earned that (top player) honor."

Loschen recalled one time, however, when he felt compelled to remove Scholz from a game.

"Dave Gehrke got married on a Saturday and I talked him into staying for our Sunday tourney game against Buckley the next day," Loschen said. "Scholz was pitching, but I put Gehrke in and he got the side out. If I'd asked him to stay and then he didn't get to pitch, his family wouldn't have thought too much of me."

Other all-time all-stars:

Ken Crawford • Thomasboro • 1991-2001
First player to win three consecutive batting titles (1993, '94 and '95); .544 mark in '95 was E.I. record and now ranks second all time; batted .412 with 249 hits in 604 at-bats.

Jeff Demith

Jeff Demith • Thomasboro • 1983-2000
Had 15 seasons of batting .300 or better and holds career record for hits; overall batted .366 with 461 hits in 1,258 at-bats.

Bill Elliott • Thomasboro • 1980-1997
Left-handed slugger won record seven home run titles, holds marks for homers in a season (13) and career (100); batted .358 with 432 hits in 1,208 at-bats.

Bill Elliott

Ehm Franzen • Flatville • 1937-1955
Records unavailable for some years but had documented mound mark of 66-28 and batted .267, with 114 hits in 427 at-bats.

Bill Gillispie • Champaign Eagles, Rantoul • 1969-1972
First player to hit at least .500 in two seasons, Chanute airman won batting titles in three of his four seasons, batted .444 with 120 hits in 270 at-bats.

Ralph Loschen • Flatville, Gifford-Flatville • 1943-1973
Complete totals not available for every season but had documented .315 average with 285 hits in 904 at-bats; managed more than 40 seasons.

Virgil Scheiwe • Buckley • 1939-1961
Only once had more than two losses in a season; for years stats were available he had 84-21 career mark and a .288 batting average (214 for 744). Managed Dutch Masters for years.

Kevin Sprau • Buckley, Rantoul, Thomasboro • 1972-1990
Set E.I. record with 125 career wins (including postseason) and 1,164 career strikeouts. Batted .309 with 202 hits in 654 at-bats.

Bill Wantland • Buckley, Thomasboro, Gifford-Flatville • 1978-1999
Known as the Pete Rose of the E.I. for sprinting out walks and head-first slides, second for hits, batting .324 with 457 hits in 1,410 at-bats.

Bill
Wantland

Honorable mention: Gary Buhr, Warren Buswell, Corey Fox, Dick Franzen, Bob Harold, John Harshbarger, Jake Krause, Dan Lathrop, Scott Lockhart, Steve Maddock, Tom Posey, Roy Radmaker, Lee Schinker, Dave Strang, Loren Tate, Ernie Westfield, John Widdersheim, Carl Wolf.

Gifford-Flatville's Gary Buhr

Mike Scholz's top 10 moments

Pitcher Mike Scholz selected 10 of his most memorable moments from his star-studded E.I. career:

1) Giving up a hit to my former coach, (Lake Land's) Gene Creek, in a game with Mattoon;
2) Hitting a home run to dead center field in Paxton;
3) Being chased by a fan after a game because he had lost a lot of money;
4) Shaking hands after a game with Fisher when I had pitched a no-hitter and one of the players was raising his hand to hit me when (catcher) Scott Rafferty tackled him;
5) Pitching to my brother Pat in the 1974 E.I. championship game;
6) Being told on a Sunday morning the day of a championship game by then-UI athletic director Cecil Coleman that I could not pitch in the E.I. tournament because of NCAA or Big Ten regulations which prohibited it;
7) Working with Scott Rafferty, the best catcher ever to throw to. We just thought alike and he was extremely competitive and smart about the game;

Catching Up

8) Every Sunday, I had to be at the top of my game because I felt like a marked man. When you are successful, then expectations are high. As competitive as the league was, all the spectators wanted to see you fail. This was extremely motivating to me to always be the very best;

9) Winning 14 titles (between regular season and tournaments);

10) Playing with Gifford-Flatville, a team that refused to lose. Players were friends on and off the field. Ralph (Loschen) and Dick (Franzen) provided leadership and worked hard recruiting good players."

Special players

Individuals who most impressed Scholz during his E.I. tenure (listed alphabetically):

BEST HITTERS

Bill Elliott • Thomasboro
Steve Maddock • Royal
Tom Posey • Buckley
Pat Prina • Paxton

Del Ryan

BEST BASE RUNNERS

Del Ryan • Rantoul
Bill Wantland • Thomasboro

John
Harshbarger

BEST PITCHERS

Bob Harold • Gifford-Flatville
John Harshbarger • Thomasboro
Dan Lathrop • Rantoul
Jerry O'Neill • Royal
Kevin Sprau • Buckley, Rantoul, Thomasboro
Steve Ward • Rantoul
John Widdersheim • Mattoon, Gifford-Flatville

Women of the E.I.

Diehard baseball fans weren't the only spectators who showed up at the ball-park for the Sunday afternoon doubleheaders.

At most locations, there was a bevy of beautiful young women. Truth is, they were probably less interested in the game than they were in the young men playing the game.

Stacey Perkinson Posey's father, Dave Perkinson, was an ardent Buckley Dutch Master fan and game day meant family day at the venerable ballpark. Dave Perkinson's interest could be traced back to watching his uncle Virgil Scheiwe (for whom the ballpark has been renamed) play and coach the Dutch Masters.

"The best part of growing up in an E.I. community is the culture and climate that is emulated," Stacey said. "As a child, the E.I. season was like the planning of a great vacation leading up to the championship weekend. We would have a weekly routine of getting our coolers of pop and beer (for my dad) ready, along with snacks and, of course, baseball mitts and balls. We would travel to the ball fields for a weekly dose of baseball education."

As a youngster, Stacey Perkinson idolized the players and made a promise to herself.

"My heart bled Buckley blue and red," she said. "To me, the players were like celebrities. I vowed as a kid I would marry a Dutch Master."

She developed an allegiance to different players, which she referred to as "boyfriends" in her mind.

"Many times, I picked the greats, Scott Lockhart, Kevin Sprau and even Billy Wantland before he left to go with Gifford-Flatville," Stacey said. "It was a place of true innocence. Children could go to the field, play, chase foul balls for a quarter and use their earnings for the best popcorn and the coldest pop in the world, and just be kids. Everyone was safe and surrounded by what is so great about small-town America."

As she grew into adulthood, Perkinson's ambition was realized.

On July 28, 2001, she was married to T.J. Posey, an infielder who played 13 seasons for Buckley. The couple, who now live in southern Illinois, had met in 1992 when T.J. Posey was a rookie with the Buckley team.

"We were friends for four years before we dated," Stacey said.

Among her wedding presents was one that might be considered expected for a tried-and-true Buckley baseball fan.

"My grandfather, Richard Hilligoss, gave me my first cowbell, which was engraved on my wedding day," Stacey said. "Ringing that bell, whether it was when the Dutch Masters took the field or at the end of the day to celebrate a win, or even the effort in defeat, always brings a smile.

In Buckley, baseball is more than a game, it's a way of life.

"It is an addictive friendship. People appreciate what this league has done for the communities and the players throughout the years.

"The players, fans, grounds crew and even the pastor were all doing the same thing on Sunday afternoon: cheering on their favorite team at the ballpark. I am proud to say that I grew up in a community where baseball was a part of your education."

E.I. LEAGUE PRESIDENTS

NAME	YEARS
Jack Waldron	1936-1957
Carl 'Hap' Parker	1958-1961
Rae Blaemire	1962-1964
Al Ellsworth	1965-1990
Marty Kirby	1991-2000
Louie Krumwiede	2001-2008
Fred Kroner	2009-2010

Veteran E.I. President Al Ellsworth, center, surrounded by his sons, both of whom played in the league. At left is Sam Ellsworth. At right is Mike Ellsworth.

Buckley Dutch Masters

The history of baseball in Buckley predates the formation of the Eastern Illinois Baseball League.

As far back as 1927, there was an organized baseball team in town, but one without an official nickname.

Several players, including Bill Janssen, Lee Klann and Walt Krumwiede, stopped by Roche's Pharmacy and spotted a sign in the front window advertising Dutch Master Cigars.

Buckley's ballpark at Charlie Martin's residence, the field which was used during the team's early years in the E.I. League.

The story goes that proprietor Remi Roche asked, "Why don't you take up the name Buckley Dutch Masters? After all, you're all Dutchmen."

For more than three-fourths of a century now, Buckley's summer baseball teams have been known as the Dutch Masters.

The organization has produced a wealth of E.I. batting, pitching and home run champions. However, the team has been in the headlines for reasons beyond the abilities of its highly-skilled ballplayers.

Arlie Seymour settled in the community in 1933. He had a passion for food (and opened a restaurant) as well as for baseball. His innovative ideas and take-charge attitude earned him the reputation as "the Bill Veeck of Buckley baseball," according to Louie Krumwiede, a former Dutch Master first baseman as well as one of the team's historians.

Seymour's promotions enticed large crowds of paying customers. A 1936 newspaper article noted that 3,300 fans were in attendance for a nine-inning game between the Dutch Masters and Flatville, a game the visitors won 3-1. His brainstorms included horse races, sheep-dog herding, parachute jumps, gate prizes, fireworks and — the ultimate pinnacle — nighttime ballgames.

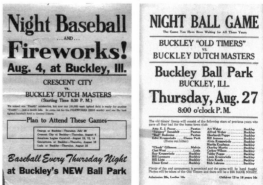

Examples of posters which Buckley produced during its early years in the E.I. League.

The team's business manager, Seymour acquired 18 floodlights from the 1933 World's Fair in Chicago. They provided Buckley the first lighted diamond in downstate Illinois outside of minor league venues.

The lights were operational until 1949. On Aug. 4 of that year, a new park was dedicated with an updated lighting system.

For youngsters, such as Louie Krumwiede, not all of the action took place between the white lines.

"I remember chasing foul balls and putting up the numbers on the new scoreboard," he said.

Fifty years later, that site — where the Dutch Masters still play their home games and still featuring a manual scoreboard — was renamed Scheiwe Field in honor of Virgil Scheiwe, whose life revolved around playing for the team or helping to maintain the field.

Available records reveal that the highest scoring game in E.I. history involved the Dutch Masters. In 1950, the team produced a 50-4 victory against Thomasboro.

Buckley's 35-hit attack was led by Bud Larson, who was 8 for 10 and scored nine runs.

Louie Krumwiede graduated from Buckley-Loda in 1959. He said the format of the league made breaking into the lineup a difficult challenge in that era.

"In those days, there was only one nine-inning game every Sunday," Krumwiede said. "Lloyd Keever was the regular first baseman, so my playing time was limited."

When Keever retired, Krumwiede's illustrious career took flight. He went on to win a batting championship in 1967, but he had one of his most memorable moments in the 1965 tournament finals against Danville.

"Dick Doran was the starting pitcher and was replaced by Emery Zimmerman in the seventh inning," Krumwiede said. "Jim Varner, our manager pinch hitting for Zimmerman, tied the game in the top of the ninth with a run-scoring double."

Once Zimmerman was removed, the Dutch Masters were short on pitching. Varner called upon Krumwiede even though, "I hadn't pitched an inning the entire season," he said.

Krumwiede not only preserved the tie, but also led off the 10th with a triple and scored what proved to be the winning run. He earned the victory by pitching a

Buckley's Louie Krumwiede and 9-month-old daughter Jill

scoreless 10th inning, ending the game with a strikeout.

Like countless players before — and after — Krumwiede's retirement as a player (in 1973) didn't end his association with the E.I. League.

"I continued to be a fan," he said. "Our children grew up at the ballpark. Our grandkids are now the ones who chase those foul balls like I did. Who knows? Maybe one of them will someday be a Dutch Master."

Krumwiede served a stint as E.I. League president (2001-2008) and stayed on as a commissioner after relinquishing the presidential duties.

"The game itself has changed," he said. "In the middle 1970s, we went from one game to doubleheaders every Sunday. The bats have changed. For years, we used wooden bats. Then, we changed to aluminum. A few years ago, when the league was down to four teams (2001), it was decided to create more interest by going back to wooden bats."

The E.I. enters its 75th season in 2010 with a seven-team wood-bat league.

"The players and teams have changed," Krumwiede said. "It used to be that every little town had a team of mostly homegrown players with a few 'outsiders' on their team.

"It was only a few miles to go to a game. Now, a team may have to go 100 miles or more for a league game. A lot of those towns no longer field a team. For those who survived, the availability of players decreased and teams had to go elsewhere to find players. This changed the level of competition to where it is today. Many of the players are current or former college players."

Krumwiede plans to remain a fan in the stands.

"Positive changes have made the league competitive as well as entertaining," he said. "There is nothing better than watching an E.I. baseball game on Sunday afternoon. E.I. baseball will be around for many years to come."

Steve Stahlman, a former Dutch Master pitcher, believes the organization has thrived because it encompassed so many more people than those in uniform.

"The American Legionnaires were the backbone of the team," Stahlman said. "They were our groundskeepers, scorekeepers, announcers, fans, ball chasers, cooks and, most of all, they were our friends. They made you feel like you were always appreciated. This, in turn, made us want to play to the best of our ability. The loyalty worked both ways. The Legionnaires worked for the team and the team worked hard to please the Legionnaires."

Game days were an event that included more than baseball.

"We did not have to worry about getting the field ready," Stahlman said. "It was ready when we got there. We warmed up for the game, played the game and then the Legionnaires would serve a picnic-style dinner for the players, wives and kids. The players could concentrate on playing the game. It was a great Sunday outing."

When he played, Stahlman said there was a high baseball IQ in the dugout.

"We had four high school coaches playing," he said. "Tom Posey coached at Crescent City. Tom Wiergatz was the coach at Sheldon. Ed Sennett was the coach at LeRoy and I was a coach at Cissna Park."

Stahlman said the coaches encouraged their prep players to join the Dutch Masters and their efforts were fruitful.

"We had enough players interested in trying out that there was talk about sponsoring two teams from Buckley," he said.

Buckley's best

With the help of some ardent Dutch Master followers, an all-time list of Buckley's greatest players was divided into an old-timer's group and a modern era all-star group. These are the 22 best for a franchise which has been in existence for all 75 years of the E.I. League:

MODERN ERA (1977-2009)

NAME	POS.	COMMENT
Kenton Carley	1B	An outstanding glove man as well as a feared hitter
Steve Ekhoff	P	Pinpoint control and an ability to work quickly were his calling cards during the '90s
Trent Eshleman	SS	An infield anchor for 15 years before becoming more manager than player
Tim Kemmer	CF	A five-tool player regarded as the best center fielder ever to play in the organization
Jake Krause	C	Known as 'the straw that stirred the drink' for more than a decade
Scott Lockhart	SS	A .370 career hitter for 14 years, amassing a club-record 374 hits
Eddie Moore	P	An unmatched desire to win made the former minor leaguer one of the team's most storied hurlers
Mark Scheiwe	1B	Most prolific fastball hitter in his era; played or coached for 20 years
Phil Scheiwe	LF	A steady player who was underrated and always delivered in the clutch
Justin Schroeder	P	An outstanding big-game performer throughout the first decade of the 2000s
Kevin Sprau	P	Won 53 games in two stints totaling eight years with the team, including three successive eight-win seasons in '84, '85 and '86

Kenton
Carley

Scott
Lockhart

Mark
Scheiwe

Phil
Scheiwe

OLD-TIMERS (1936-76)

NAME	POS.	COMMENT
Jerry Ditman	3B	Buckley native contributed equally in the field and at the plate; team's top hitter in 1958
Joe Dwyer	C	A power hitter who played multiple positions and also served a stint as manager
Tom Hull	C	A prolific home run hitter during his 18-year career and also the team's batting leader three straight years ('42, '43 and '44)
Herb Kaufmann	1B/P	The left-hander was the team's top hitter three straight years ('54, '55 and '56)
Mark Kaufmann	INF/P	Buckley native was the team's top hitter in both 1937 and '40
Butch Kemmer	SS	A notorious bad-ball hitter, and the E.I. batting champion in 1969; also the team leader in '58
Ed Knueppel	C	Former House of David player had a strong arm, outstanding speed and was a long-ball threat
Louie Krumwiede	1B	A 14-year veteran who won the E.I. batting crown in 1967
Tom Posey	2B	Won two batting championships in a three-year span (1974 and '76)
Virgil Scheiwe	P	Known as 'Mr. Dutch Master,' he led the league in pitching (9-1) and was third in batting (.456) in '52
Bill Weisenbarn	2B	Versatile player handy with the glove and his team's top hitter in 1962

Year-by-year Buckley batting leaders:

YEAR	NAME	AB	R	H	AVG.
1936	Ed Knueppel	82	31	36	.439
1937	Mark Kaufmann	56	13	18	.321
1938	Tom Hull	69	10	22	.319
1939	Arno Krumwiede	72	11	25	.347
1940	Mark Kaufmann	54	15	20	.370
1941	Not available	n/a	n/a	n/a	n/a
1942	Tom Hull	40	11	16	.400
1943	Tom Hull	54	11	19	.352
1944	Tom Hull	n/a	n/a	n/a	n/a
1945	Francis Gleason	42	8	16	.381
1946	Bud Larson	53	n/a	20	.377
1947	Carl Wolf	52	20	28	.538
1948	Ed Knueppel	41	12	16	.390

1949	Beryl Luecke	65	16	28	.431
1950	Virgil Scheiwe	55	17	18	.327
1951	Lloyd Inkster	44	10	17	.386
1952	Virgil Scheiwe	57	12	26	.456
1953	Russ Drechsler	64	17	28	.438
1954	Herb Kaufmann	41	10	16	.390
1955	Herb Kaufmann	27	4	9	.333
1956	Herb Kaufmann	54	14	25	.463
1957	Virgil Scheiwe	41	10	19	.463
1958	Jerry Ditman	50	15	16	.320
1959	Bill Weisenbarn	59	16	16	.271
1960	Bill Weisenbarn	58	25	24	.414
1961	Russ Drechsler	45	n/a	16	.356
1962	Bill Weisenbarn	46	n/a	15	.336
1963	Joe Dwyer	50	14	18	.360
1964	Louie Krumwiede	52	9	17	.327
1965	Stan Swearingen	19	6	8	.421
1966	Gordie Hull	38	13	17	.447
1967	Louie Krumwiede	44	10	20	.455
1968	Butch Kemmer	51	16	20	.392
1969	Butch Kemmer	21	4	10	.476
1970	Joe Dwyer	14	4	6	.429
1971	Stan Feller	63	16	26	.413
1972	Gordie Hull	94	21	36	.383
1972	Mick Larson	94	22	36	.383
1973	Gary Rabe	26	7	13	,500
1974	Tom Posey	54	18	27	.500
1975	Rick Hull	53	9	18	.340
1976	Tom Posey	75	22	36	.480
1977	Scott Lockhart	90	25	36	.400
1978	Scott Lockhart	93	27	38	.409

1979	Bill Wantland	66	10	23	.348
1980	Scott Lockhart	67	16	30	.448
1981	Scott Lockhart	65	16	23	.354
1982	Will Weinhorst	43	5	16	,372
1983	Phil Scheiwe	107	23	39	.364
1984	Troy Genzel	79	6	28	.354
1985	Kenton Carley	84	22	36	.429
1986	Eddie Moore	46	9	23	.500
1987	Dave Gibson	93	23	37	.398
1988	Eric LaVoie	75	15	32	.427
1989	Mark Scheiwe	62	22	23	.359
1990	Tim Kemmer	65	20	32	.492
1991	Trent Eshleman	65	17	28	.431
1992	Dave Gibson	55	15	24	.436
1993	Ty Nicol	43	16	17	.395
1994	Jerry Farris	42	11	18	.429
1995	Jake Krause	67	9	27	.403
1996	Tom Waldrop	55	19	31	.564
1997	Jake Krause	77	20	33	.429
1998	Terry McDevitt	48	20	21	.438
1999	Nate Henrichs	62	15	28	.452
2000	Joel Dodson	29	6	12	.414
2001	Jake Krause	61	14	28	.426
2002	Jake Krause	77	25	35	.455
2003	Chris Hawkins	38	n/a	13	.342
2004	Blake Schoonover	99	29	48	.485
2005	Ryne Scheiwe	50	15	19	.380
2006	T.J. Posey	44	7	17	.386
2007	Kevin Wyman	53	10	19	.358
2008	Kevin Wyman	47	18	23	.489
2009	Bryce Redeker	61	15	19	.311

Catching Up

Year-by-year Buckley pitching leaders:

YEAR	NAME	RECORD	YEAR	NAME	RECORD
1936	Elmer Bultman	n/a	1974	Kevin Sprau	6-3
1937	Elmer Bultman	n/a	1975	Steve Stahlman	5-4
1938	Pete Wagner	10-9	1976	Steve Stahlman	10-2
1939	Pete Wagner	5-7	1977	Steve Stahlman	10-3
1940	Walter 'Lefty' House	11-4	1978	Steve Stahlman	6-1
1941	Howard Marten	6-1	1979	Not available	n/a
1942	Erv Sprehe	1-1	1980	Ed Sennett	7-2
1943	Not available	n/a	1981	Will Weinhorst	7-1
1944	Not available	n/a	1982	Will Weinhorst	9-3
1945	Marvin Stiegman	4-3	1983	Will Weinhorst	8-2
1946	Virgil Scheiwe	11-2	1984	Kevin Sprau	7-4
1947	Lloyd Inkster	4-2	1985	Eric LaVoie	9-4
1947	Virgil Scheiwe	4-2	1986	Eddie Moore	4-2
1948	Arlyn Lober	5-2	1987	Eric LaVoie	5-1
1949	Marvin Stiegman	8-3	1988	Eddie Moore	11-3
1950	Ken Sturm	6-1	1989	Eddie Moore	8-3
1951	Virgil Scheiwe	6-2	1990	Andy Cotner	4-0
1952	Virgil Scheiwe	9-1	1991	Mike Walling	7-0
1953	Virgil Scheiwe	8-1	1992	Todd Post	7-2
1954	Not available	n/a	1993	Steve Ekhoff	8-2
1955	Virgil Scheiwe	4-1	1993	Jason Garrelts	8-2
1956	Herb Kaufmann	7-1	1994	Steve Ekhoff	7-4
1957	Virgil Scheiwe	9-1	1995	Steve Ekhoff`	10-1
1958	Virgil Scheiwe	10-2	1996	Steve Ekhoff	11-2
1959	Dick Doran	7-1	1997	Troy Elias	7-0
1960	Dick Doran	6-2	1997	Jason Garrelts	7-0
1961	Dick Doran	5-3	1998	Jake Zajc	7-1
1962	Dick Doran	4-4	1999	P.J. Moore	4-0
1963	Dick Doran	3-3	1999	Brent Niebuhr	4-0
1964	Dick Freehill	3-4	2000	Brent Niebuhr	5-2
1965	Dick Doran	4-3	2001	Justin Schroeder	8-1
1966	Mick Larson	6-3	2002	Justin Schroeder	4-0
1967	Mick Larson	8-4	2003	Justin Schroeder	7-2
1968	Not available	n/a	2004	Andy Goodrich	5-2
1969	Dick Doran	5-2	2005	Justin Schroeder	7-0
1970	Dick Doran	4-4	2006	Brock Niebuhr	6-0
1971	Mick Larson	5-6	2007	Justin Schroeder	6-0
1972	Kevin Sprau	6-0	2008	Jacob Stauffenberg	5-0
1973	Kevin Sprau	7-2	2009	Tyler Ware	6-1

The 1930s

1936

The first year, and the teams and managers:

Buckley, Arlie Seymour

Chanute Field, Capt. J.E. Duke, Jr.

Flatville, John Franzen

Leverett, Howard Eaton

Rankin, R.J. Christiansen

Royal, John D. Grussing

Sadorus, Ernest Doehring

Seymour, Clark Thomas

Thomasboro, Joe Maier

106th Cavalry, R.C. Van Duyn

Commissioners:

Jack Waldron, President

Shelby Himes, Secretary

Elvin 'Dock' Leedy

Flatville was the undisputed top team, winning the regular season title with a 15-2 record and following up with a tournament crown. The team missed by one year, however, of a feat which has never happened during the "official" existence of the E.I.

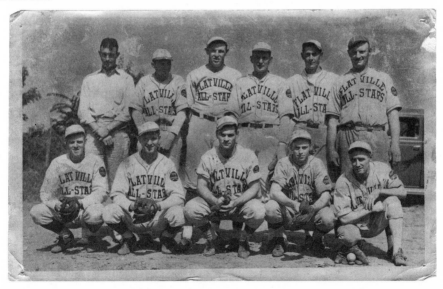

Flatville's 1937 runner-up team. From row, from left, are: George Johnson, Ehm Franzen, Wallie Kimberlin, Ralph Hayes and Pat Patterson. Back row, from left, are: Al Huls, Ike Yount, Henry Sjuts, George Roelfs, Herman Selsor and John Franzen.

Catching Up

Flatville's 1935 team won every regular season game it played. Through 2009, no team has ever escaped an entire season without at least one loss.

1937

The Champaign Plumbers, led by batting champion Noel Pike, started their late-decade dynasty by sweeping both regular season and tournament crowns. It was the first of three consecutive league titles, won or shared.

1938

The Champaign Plumbers won both the regular season and tournament titles. The team's tournament roster: Elba Bales, Roy Beckett, Robert Blaisdell, Harry Combes, Max Craig, Walt Flanigan, Jack Fuzak, William Fuzak, H.E. Freeman, Harold Grierson, Lloyd Hopkins, Max Pike, Cy Vaughn and Dwight Wilkey. The team was coached by Andy Grierson.

Combes, the future UI men's basketball coach, was the league's top hitter.

1939

Seymour's appropriately named Dill Seymour capped his season with a 7 for 7 performance that lifted his batting average to .453 and enabled him to win the batting title. Royal's Glenn Reeves was the runner-up (.410).

Monticello's Lloyd Hopkins set a strikeout record (155) that stood for 25 years.

The 1940s

1940

Ivesdale became the first — and only — team to finish last during the regular season and then rebound to win the tournament. Ivesdale was 10th in the 10-team league, which was won by Buckley.

Catcher Albert 'Ab' Harshbarger and third baseman Joe Doyle, who had graduated from Bement High School earlier in the year, led the stunning postseason romp.

Ivesdale edged Flatville 11-10 in the semifinals and then upended Thomasboro 8-4 to win the tournament.

1941

The Champaign Plumbers, who became the first team with back-to-back tournament championships starting in 1938, became the first to win three postseason crowns in 1941. After the first decade of the E.I.'s existence, the Plumbers were the only program with more than one tournament title.

1942

Year 7 of the E.I. resulted in the first two-time batting champion and the first person to hit at least .500 for the season. Seymour's Dill Seymour, the 1939 batting titlist, earned a second crown and compiled a .516 average.

Unlike in 1939, when the Champaign Plumbers and Seymour tied for regular season supremacy with 15-3 records, the teams which shared first place had a one-game playoff to determine the champion. Royal (11-2) won the playoff, 7-3, over Seymour (10-3).

Seymour, however, regrouped and won its first tournament title.

1943

This year marked the first — and through 74 years, the only — time that the batting champion didn't hit over .400. Flatville's John Flessner won the title with a .381 average. The next lowest average for a batting titlist was .410 by Willie Southall, from the Champaign Eagles, in 1970.

1944

Chanute Air Force Base, in Rantoul, won its first and only regular season title (finishing at 12-2, one game in front of Royal) as well as its first and only tournament title. Dick Newell won eight games and was the team's ace. Chanute had its only batting champion, Bryan Howell, who hit .468.

Chanute, which wasn't in the league in 1943, did not return in 1945 to defend its title. In all, the base had an E.I. entry nine years between 1936 — when it was one of the league's 10 charter members — and 1965.

1945

Seymour's regular season co-champions teamed up for a .336 batting average, then an E.I. record. Seymour and Royal shared top honors for the regular season. It was 37 more years before the team batting average record for a season was broken by Thomasboro.

1946

1946 All-Stars:

Catcher, Glenn Reeves, Royal

First base, Ed Wickland, Campus Legion

Second base, Don Cribbett, Royal

Shortstop, Ralph Loschen, Flatville

Third base, Del Montgerard, Danville

Left field, Harm Frerichs, Royal

Center field, (tie) Francis Gleason, Buckley, and Charles Hursey, Champaign Colts

Right field, Gerald Hutchcraft, Seymour

Pitcher, Warren Buswell, Seymour

Flatville won the 1946 tournament crown on Sept. 8 topping Buckley 10-2 in the finals at Gifford. Ike Yount was the winning pitcher and also had three hits. Mike Franzen's run-scoring single snapped a 2-2 tie and ignited Flatville's eight-run eighth inning.

Squad members in uniform that day for Flatville: Eldred Bergman, Art Busboom, Ben Chambliss, Howard Eaton, Harry Flessner, Dick Franzen, Ehm Franzen, Mike Franzen, Herb Johnson, Ralph Loschen, Wilbur Kopmann and Ike Yount. The team was managed by John Franzen. The scorekeeper was Don Curtis and the batboy was Norman Franzen.

1947

Led by shortstop Bud Larson, who was 8 for 10 and scored nine runs, Buckley set an E.I. record by battering Thomasboro 50-4. The Dutch Masters scored at least one run in all nine innings of the May 3 game, with a high of 16 in the fourth inning.

A subsequent newspaper article stated, "the hardest working man there was Len Ecker, scorekeeper."

Catcher Ed Knuepple hit a grand slam in the fourth inning. According to a published report, when he batted for the final time in the inning, he didn't remove his shin pads.

Seymour, fifth in the regular season, outscored Buckley 16-9 to win the post-season tournament. Seymour's roster: John Apperson, Al Attrogge, Hoot Beckett, Warren Buswell, Harvey Ditter, Don Gordon, Al Herges, Gerald Hutchcraft, Carl Hillman, Wallie Kimberlin, Bud Merryman, Lyle Nelson, Joe Pfeffer, Lyman Pitcher, Jim Vancil, Lou Wheeler, Arnold Young and Forrest Young. Pfeffer was the team's coach.

1948

Royal's roster when it won the tournament championship: Glen Busboom, Don Cribbett, John Flessner, Jack Franklin, Harm Frerichs, Henry Miller, Henry Osterbur, Herb Osterbur, Robert Osterbur, Bill Parks, Skeeter Roughton and Verne Wienke. The coaches were Bob Hunter and Red Freeman, and the batboy was Irvin Buhr.

1949

Workhorse Ehm Franzen pitched the distance for Flatville in the opening game of a doubleheader, losing to Buckley 1-0. He returned for an encore and hurled another complete game, winning 4-3. For the 18 innings, he struck out 27 batters and yielded eight hits.

The 1950s

1950

One of the league's most controversial games took place on June 4 at Gifford. In a showdown between unbeatens, Flatville edged Loda 2-1 behind the pitching of Ehm Franzen.

After the game, Loda catcher Eldred 'Bumps' Hadley and teammate D.D. Foote drove back to Gifford to measure the distance from the pitching mound to the plate. They found it to be 57 feet, 6 inches, not the mandatory 60-6. A day later, Loda manager Chet West filed a protest. An E.I. commissioner verified the distance and ordered the game replayed.

Flatville manager John Franzen decided to pull his team out of the league rather than correct the problem. A game against Sidney on June 11 was not played, and was followed by a rainout the following week.

E.I. commissioners never acted on the withdrawal and Flatville fans — as well as players, including Ehm Franzen — pressured John Franzen into relenting.

The game was replayed on July 13 with an estimated 1,500 spectators in attendance. Loda touched Ehm Franzen for five first-inning runs and held on for a 5-3 decision.

Loda went on to capture E.I. regular season laurels with a 16-2 record. Flatville ended fourth at 10-5, including a forfeit loss to Sidney (its only win) for the game not played.

The last laugh, however, belonged to Flatville, which won the tournament crown with a 12-5 decision against Loda.

Flatville's 1950 tournament champions were managed by John Franzen, who was assisted by Al Herges. Squad members included Moe Dodds, Dick Franzen, Ehm Franzen, Mike Franzen, Jack Herbert, Gerald Hutchcraft, Herb Johnson, Ralph Loschen, Don Miles, Dick Squire, Dick Weissman and Dale Williams. Harm Frerichs was the scorekeeper.

1951

Mother Nature was the early-season winner. All Week 1 games were rained out, as were all Week 2 games. In order to get all of the postponed games played, a planned midseason tournament was canceled.

Once the action got going, Flatville lost just once in 14 games while winning the regular season title. The team was the first to go through the season with only one loss.

1951 All-Stars:

    Catcher, Eldred 'Bumps' Hadley, Loda
    First base, Herb Kaufmann, Buckley
    Second base, Elmer Weber, Buckley
    Shortstop, Gus Skizas, Champaign

Third base, Ray Ehler, Flatville
Left field, Pete Inkster, Buckley
Center field, Russ Drechsler, Loda
Right field, Bob Ems, Thomasboro
Pitcher, Ehm Franzen, Flatville

1952

Thomasboro's Bob Ems was the first person to win back-to-back batting championships. A year after hitting .500, he repeated with a .485 average.

Buckley matched Flatville's 13-1 record for the previous season, but it was not the start of a league-wide trend. It would be 27 more years before a team suffered just one regular season loss.

1953

An exhibition game on May 30 was set up to inaugurate the Knights of Columbus baseball field on West Springfield Ave., Champaign, about a mile west of Mattis Ave.

The 1953 UI team, which had shared the Big Ten title with Michigan, faced an assortment of E.I. all-stars coached by Royal's Don Cribbett (the 1945 batting champion).

The UI opened with Clive Follmer on the mound and the E.I. countered with Ehm Franzen.

The Illini built a 3-0 lead before Franzen pounded a game-tying three-run homer — the only hit allowed by Follmer. Illinois regained control again, 6-3, thanks to a pair of home runs by Ron Ultes.

The E.I. went ahead to stay in the fifth, 7-6, with the go-ahead run being scored by Ralph Loschen on a double by Royal's Dick Foster. Reliever Virgil Scheiwe earned the win and received breathing room when Buckley catcher Eldred 'Bumps' Hadley belted a grand slam.

"My season was over and it was a good game. All the seats were taken," said Lee Eilbracht, the second-year Illini coach. "I pinch hit and hit what I thought was a homer, but it curved foul. The E.I. had good players. Scheiwe was a heck of a pitcher. He should have been in pro ball. He was very, very fast."

The E.I.'s 12-7 victory against the Big Ten co-champions was regaled 25 years later by *News-Gazette* sports writer E.W. Hesse, who labeled it, "one of the glory days in the long and storied past of the E.I."

1953 managers:
Buckley, Ed Yonke
Champaign Eagles, Ray Hines and Wardell Jackson
Flatville, Harm Frerichs and Ralph Loschen
Ivesdale, John Radmaker
Knights of Columbus, Al Herges
Monticello, Loren Tate and Ecus Vaughn
Rantoul, Sam Good and Ted Siddens
Royal, Don Cribbett and Lorenz Busboom

Commissioners:
Jack Waldron, President
Bill Burrows, Treasurer
Shelby Himes, Secretary
Al Nelson
Carl 'Hap' Parker

1954

Jim Freeman, from the Champaign Knights, was the first person to win outright home run titles in back-to-back years. He slugged five to take league honors. The top home run hitting team was Monticello with 10.

1955

Thanks to Chanute Air Force Base, the Rantoul entry fielded a team that featured seven airmen among the nine starters.

Right-hander Art Goreham was the pitching ace for Monticello, which topped Flatville 4-1 in the tournament championship game on Sept. 11 at Buckley. Goreham finished the year with a 15-1 record for a team that finished 17-3. He pitched Monticello past Buckley 10-1 in the semifinals and returned 90 minutes later for the title tilt and fired a nine-inning three-hitter, matching his performance against the Dutch Masters. Goreham was staked to a 1-0 second-inning lead when Loren Tate's single drove in Jim Freeman. Against Buckley, Charlie Due was 4 for 4.

For the day, Goreham fanned 18 batters, 11 in the finals against a Flatville team that had UI athletes Paul and Phil Judson (about to start their senior season in basketball with the Illini) in the lineup. In the semis, Goreham carried a no-hitter into the ninth, but it was broken up by Leonard Hull's single.

Monticello's tournament roster: Charlie Due, Clyde Foster, Jim Freeman, Alfred Gadbury, Rich Gadbury, Art Goreham, Roy Phillips, Paul Schimanski, Bud Smith, Bill Sprague, Gene Stratman, Loren Tate, Don Winter, Bob York and Jim York. Ecus Vaughn was the coach.

1956

Monticello was unable to even try and defend its title. When first-round tourney games were played on Aug. 19 Monticello was unable to field nine players and forfeited to the Champaign-Urbana Colts.

The Champaign Knights beat Royal in the tournament finals.

The Knights' tournament roster: Harlan Clausen, Don Diller, Charlie Due, Fred Gleason, Jim Gannaway, Kenny Grubb, Ken Hearn, Jerry McKinney, Bob Madix, Jim McNabney, Dick Ogdon, Dick 'Rocky' Raklovits, Sam Rebecca, Bill Busch, Bob Slade and Bob Wiman. Al Herges was the manager.

1957

Villa Grove was ordered to forfeit a tournament victory against the Champaign Knights after a ruling that it had used an ineligible player. Catcher Jim Prosser, who hit a three-run homer with two outs in the bottom of the eighth inning in Villa Grove's 4-3 on-field victory, had started the season playing for Newman but left that team after one week.

Villa Grove added him at midseason but never obtained a written release. Thus, he was still considered a member of Newman's roster despite having played the latter half of the season with Villa Grove.

Villa Grove manager Clarence Riddle argued that no one objected when he submitted his tournament roster in advance and it had Prosser's name included.

News-Gazette sports writer Bill Schrader reported in the Sept. 4 editions that, "the argument continued for two hours," before a ruling against Villa Grove placed the Knights into the semifinal round.

The Knights took advantage, advancing to the title game, where they lost to Gifford-Flatville, 7-4.

1958

Loren Tate, of the Champaign Knights, fired a perfect game to open the season on April 27. He struck out 16 in a seven-inning game, a 20-0 victory against Ivesdale. It was the league's second perfect game and first since one pitched by Seymour's Warren Buswell in 1946. Tate went on to win both batting and pitching titles that summer, marking the first double-double in E.I. history. Tate batted .489. On the mound, he was 14-1.

Ironically, in 1957, while pitching for Ivesdale, Tate had pitched a no-hitter.

His double-double feat was matched by Roy Radmaker, of the Champaign Eagles, in 1964. Radmaker batted .526, still the fourth-highest average in E.I. history, and had a 7-1 pitching record.

Roy Radmaker

Tate's first-game heroics in 1958 overshadowed another outstanding pitching performance on the same day, Loda's Don Hackerson recorded 21 strikeouts in a 6-5 win against Cissna Park.

1959

For the first time in league history, the batting crown wasn't worn by just one person. Three athletes shared top honors after getting hits in half of their at-bats. Sharing the title were Cliff Adkinson, from the Champaign Eagles, who was 26 for 52; Loda's Butch Kemmer who was 16 for 32; and Gifford-Flatville's Norm Franzen who was also 16 for 32.

Royal's Ken Fletcher won the home run title and became the answer to a trivia question: Which E.I. player went the longest between home run titles? Fifteen years later, Fletcher shared the 1974 home run trophy with Gibson City's Warren Cox.

Stars of the 1950s

Ehm Franzen

The first year for the Eastern Illinois Baseball League was the first season for a teenager from Flatville to play amateur baseball in an adult league.

Ehm Franzen was a right-handed pitcher whose reputation and record spoke for themselves and resonated success.

A familiar question was posed to Franzen during the years he dominated E.I. hitters.

"So many guys said, 'Why didn't you go to the big leagues?'" Franzen said.

The answer was simple.

"Money talks," he said.

Franzen said he had a minor league contract offer from the Brooklyn Dodgers for $180 a month, but he felt obligated to turn it down. He had an

Brothers Ehm Franzen, left, and Dick Franzen

excavating and construction business and said with his bulldozer, "I could make that in three days."

For 20 years, Franzen was one of the E.I.'s premier hurlers.

Often throwing to his brother, Dick, who was 2 years younger, Ehm Franzen established a lasting legacy.

He opened the 1944 season for Flatville with a no-hitter in a 23-0 win against rival Gifford. A year later, on May 27, 1945, he tossed a no-hitter against the Illini Vets, fanning 13 and facing one batter over the minimum in his 1-0 nine-inning triumph.

The lone run was driven in by his cousin, first baseman Mike Franzen, whose first-inning single plated Jim Bayne.

In an era when teams played single games — unless a rain-out created a doubleheader — Ehm Franzen showed his tenacity and durability later in the summer of '45.

The 25-year-old pitched all 18 innings in a split with Buckley, holding the visiting Dutch Masters scoreless in one 12-inning stretch. He struck out 27 for the twin bill, losing the opener 1-0 and winning the nightcap 4-3. For the day, he permitted eight hits.

"The next morning," Franzen said, "my father-in-law came over to see if I was sore and in bed, but I was down the lane cutting weeds. That doubleheader is one of my best memories."

He said he and his brother communicated well as the battery. If they suspected opposing teams were catching the signs, they took action.

The field at Royal on June 18, 1961, when the home team defeated the touring Kansas City Monarchs and Satchel Paige, 7-6, in an exhibition game.

"He knew if they'd holler (fastball) to watch out, I'd cross them up and a curve would be coming," Ehm Franzen said.

As youngsters, the boys played pitch and catch at every opportunity.

"After supper, we'd be in the front yard and my mother would say, 'You're making a hole in the lawn,'" Ehm Franzen recalled.

The pitcher enjoyed his most productive seasons after he'd played in the E.I. for a dozen years. He had a 13-2 record in 1949 and a 13-1 mark in 1951.

The win totals today are tied for third on the E.I. single-season charts, a position he shares with Seymour's Wallie Kimberlin (13-2 in 1939).

In a 1951 story, *News-Gazette* sport editor Jack Prowell wrote about Franzen, "when he was in his prime, there was no one in the league with any pitch that was harder."

Franzen quipped, however, that his fastball might not have been the quickest in his family.

"Dick could throw the ball back to you faster than you could to him," Ehm Franzen said.

As he aged, Ehm Franzen relied less on velocity and more on a knuckleball he had developed. In the interview with Prowell, he spoke about how tempting some of his offerings were.

"Sometimes," he said, "they look so good that I'd like to bat against them myself."

Franzen's third E.I. no-hitter came in 1952 in a 6-0 Week 2 win against an Ivesdale team that featured Loren Tate as the shortstop and leadoff hitter. Eldred Bergman and Ralph Loschen led Flatville's 11-hit attack with 3 for 5 performances against Jerry Gallivan.

Franzen was the starting pitcher in a 1948 All-Star Game where one of his teammates was future major leaguer Dick Hyde, who was playing for Fisher's first-year E.I. entry.

Catching Up

A decade later, Hyde was pitching for the Washington Senators and finished 12th in the Most Valuable Player voting in the American League following a season when his earned run average was 1.75.

Franzen estimated he won more than 100 games in his pitching career. Of those, 66 were in regular season contests. Some of his memorable moments, however, occurred in non-league exhibitions.

In a June, 1949 relief stint against Ford's of Bloomington, Franzen fanned the first 12 batters he faced and 14 of 15 overall in Flatville's 12-4 triumph. As a point of reference, the major league record for consecutive strikeouts by a pitcher is 10 and was set by the Mets' Tom Seaver in 1970.

Franzen pitched two exhibitions where he was matched against legendary Satchel Paige, who in 1948 helped the Cleveland Indians win the World Series.

The second matchup came in Royal in 1961 when the 41-year-old Franzen ended a four-year retirement to throw against the touring Kansas City Monarchs. "I struck out Paige," Franzen said, "and we won, 7-6."

Dick Franzen

Dick Franzen, who farmed and worked for Illiana Construction, was also a top-notch bowler. He played for Flatville, batting .340 in 1945 (eighth in the league) and later joined Ralph Loschen as co-coaches. During an 11-year stretch from 1973 to '84, their Gifford-Flatville teams won 15 regular season or tournament championships.

After Franzen's death at age 87 on Nov. 10, 2009, Loschen recalled memories of his former colleague for a *News-Gazette* article that was published Dec. 27, 2009.

What follows are Loschen's comments for the newspaper article as well as additional thoughts which were edited out of the original version for space reasons.

"We knew each other from when we were kids. He went to Gifford, McMasters Elementary School. I went to Flatville Grade School. I had to walk a mile and a quarter every day to go to school. Dick had to walk about a mile. That's how we got our legs in shape.

"I got to know him through baseball. We ended up being related. I married a Franzen, and my wife and Dick were second cousins. When we got married in 1946, they (Dick and his wife Irene) stood up for us. We got married on a Saturday and instead of going on a honeymoon, which very few people did in those days, we played Royal the next day.

"He was a pretty tough ball player. His fingers were banged up from all those years of catching. He caught Dizzy Dean and I played third base (when Dean played a game for Flatville in 1955). He caught his brother, Ehm.

"Dick was a daring baseball player. He wasn't scared of anything. He always liked to steal bases. We played in Danville for a long time with the Square Deal team, coached by Andy Cohen.

"After we were done playing, we coached together for more than 30 years. He was my third base coach. When we started, it was just called Flatville. In the 1970s, we bought the field (along with three other individuals, Loschen's son Norlyn, Loschen's sister Dorothy and long time Gifford-Flatville supporter Joe Lamb).

"We spent a lot of time at the park mowing and doing things to improve it. We put a new fence in the outfield, new dugouts, the pavilion. Everything out there, Dick and I were involved in.

"For some reason or another, I still think Dick will call me. We would discuss things and plan what we were going to do. It will be hard to go to the ballpark and not have him there."

Dave Strang, who played second base for the Giflats from 1976 to 1988, said Loschen and Franzen were the rocks that held the team together.

Ralph Loschen   Dick Franzen

"They provided the tradition and background for the team and league," Strang said. "They treated us extremely well and made it fun to play. Ralph was in charge of getting players and he was always working to get the best players so we could remain very competitive. I really appreciated that because you knew we would be able to compete for the league and tournament championships every year."

Strang hopes a new generation of people step up to fill the void when both Loschen and Franzen are gone.

"If not for people like them, the league would have already folded," Strang said. "Because of them, many people have gotten to continue their playing careers. For the E.I.'s sake, I hope there are some people who will come along with this 'love for the game' and keep the league going."

Veteran Giflat managers

Ralph Loschen started managing the Flatville baseball team in 1952. Dick Franzen joined him in 1960. They had nearly three decades together in the dugout.

Highlights of the years where one or both managed the Giflats:

YEAR	RECORD	PLACE	TOP HITTER	TOP PITCHER
1952	9-6	4th	Ken Wilk, .467	Ehm Franzen, 8-4
1953	6-8	4th (tie)	Elzer Marks, .439	Ehm Franzen, 4-5
1954	12-2	1st	Ford Leach, .361	Not available
1955	10-8	4th (tie)	Phil Judson, .333	Elmer Koestner, 3-2
1956	9-5	3rd	Roger Blaemire, .390	John Loschen, 4-0
1957	12-6	4th	Bob Christensen, .422	Ron Franzen, 5-3
				Dale Williams, 5-3
1958	13-3	2nd	Bob Christensen, .403	Ron Franzen, 3-2
1959	13-3	1st (tie)	Norm Franzen, .500	Loren Tate, 8-1
1960	9-6	7th (tie)	Marty Eichelberger, .444	Ron Franzen, 3-2
				Rick Greenfield, 3-2
1961	11-3	2nd	Tom McDevitt, .444	Rick Greenfield, 7-1
1962	8-6	3rd	Tom McDevitt, .355	Rick Greenfield, 5-3
1963	7-7	5th	Ralph Loschen, .297	Gary Meneley, 7-4
1964	9-6	2nd (tie)	Leon Busboom, .419	Andy Allen, 3-1
1965	11-4	2nd	Gayle Franzen, .400	Larry Bundy, 9-2

1966	8-7	3rd (tie)	Norlyn Loschen, .378	Brian Zimmerman, 4-3
1967			Not in league	
1968			Not in league	
1969			Not in league	
1970	5-10	6th	Larry Bundy, .339	Chip Eaton, 5-7
1971	9-8	3rd	Ken Barenthin, .358	Larry Bundy, 3-0
1972	11-19	5th	Willie Southall, .357	Norlyn Loschen, 6-4
1973	18-6	1st	Ken Barenthin, .500	Norlyn Loschen, 7-2
1974	16-4	1st (tie)	Jan South, .414	Mike Scholz, 10-1
1975	15-5	3rd	Norlyn Loschen, .361	Mike Scholz, 7-2
1976	20-3	1st	Renard Danenhower, .417	Mike Scholz, 12-0
1977	17-9	3rd	Jon Siron, .474	Mike Scholz, 10-2
1978	21-5	1st	Dave Strang, .409	Mike Scholz, 8-1
1979	23-1	1st	Dave Strang, .429	Mike Scholz, 10-0
1980	18-4	1st	Scott Rafferty, .436	Mike Scholz, 7-2
1981	17-5	1st	Mark McElwain, .429	Bruce Scheidegger, 7-2
1982	16-8	2nd	Tim Gasparich, .347	Mike Scholz, 5-0
1983	25-7	1st (tie)	Mark McElwain, .371	John Widdersheim, 12-1
1984	17-11	2nd	Dave Rear, .394	John Widdersheim, 8-3
1985	16-12	4th (tie)	Randy Harpster, .397	John Widdersheim, 6-3
1986	16-12	4th	Bill Wantland, .395	Greg Rogers, 7-6
1987	15-13	4th (tie)	Mark McElwain, .394	Greg Rogers, 6-3
1988	13-15	5th	Dave Strang, .373	Bill Lamkey, 5-3
1989	14-10	3rd	Greg Fitzgerald, .362	Marc Daniels, 7-4
1990	15-9	2nd	Chris Hammack, .314	Bob Harold, 6-4
1991			Did not manage	
1992	12-10	4th	Brent Vinson, .451	Greg 'Chip' Immke, 4-1
1993	19-3	1st	Jeff Spisok, .434	Bob Harold, 9-1
1994	12-12	4th (tie)	Ken Whited, .305	Greg Harrier, 7-3
1995			Did not manage	
1996	10-12	5th	Justin Busche, .306	Bob Harold, 6-4

NOTE: Career regular season record of 537-293 for 40 years is winning percentage of 64.7. There were 35 winning, and 11 regular season championship seasons.

Loren Tate

Long before he was the foremost authority on University of Illinois sports, particularly football and men's basketball, Loren Tate was gaining a reputation as one of the top all-around baseball players in the E.I. In 1958, he captured both the league batting and pitching crowns in the same season.

Loren Tate

Norlyn Loschen

Greg Fitzgerald

His story, told in his words, is one which illustrates the value of perseverance.

"It is the nature of things that star athletes who play at major collegiate or professional levels tend to look other directions when their playing days are over. For example, you wouldn't expect Clive Follmer, a fastballing Big Ten mound ace during my bench-sitting days at the UI, to continue play. Nor Dick Hyde, the submarine hurler who reached the majors. They got their fill.

"I was different. Despite my pleadings to coach John Freemuth, I never got to pitch an inning at Monticello High School. And, I didn't work my way to the mound until the early 1950s after Ecus Vaughn and I put together a Monticello team in the E.I. League.

"Even then, Ecus had to be convinced. Truth is, I wasn't any good and he kept reminding me of that fact. So did my manager, Roy Vail, in Schererville, Ind., after I moved north in the mid-1950s.

"But I guess I wanted to play more than anybody you know. Why else would I still be playing softball at age 77 this past summer (2009)? If I'm counting correctly, that old-timer Busey gang in 2009 was the 39th team I've played for, and some for 10 years or more. In some cases, I played for two or three teams at the same time, some with disastrous results.

"Going back, several things happened. I was a slow developer. I finally grew from 145 pounds to 175. And, I had a gimmick. I learned to throw a curve by twisting the ball into my hand and withholding my thumb (it's called cunny-thumbing) and over time, I threw it from the top (for a drop), sidearm and, with two strikes, underhanded. My 'trick pitch' was my fastball. It wasn't expected. This would never have worked at the professional level, but once-a-week hitters had difficulty timing those sweeping curves.

"Then, too, I was pitching mid-week in Hammond, Ind., and on Sundays in the E.I. League for, over the years, Monticello, Ivesdale, the Champaign Knights and Gifford-Flatville. Truth is, I had a rubber arm. I threw several doubleheaders and, unbeknownst to my managers on one occasion, I pitched full games three days in a row. That actually happened in 1958 when I was with Al Herges' Knights. It was a special year in which, technically speaking and maybe it's a stretch, I didn't allow an earned run in my first five Knights' games, threw a perfect game against Ivesdale, and finished 14-1.

"As for winning the batting title, that was just a case of a mature guy with good hand-eye coordination finding some holes. I could always make contact, but without a lot of power.

"I quit playing in the E.I. when I joined a Sunday league in Lansing, Ill. Less traveling. In 1963, nearing my 32nd birthday, I was named the state's top amateur pitcher in the 16-team state tournament in Elgin, and twice pitched in the national tournament in Wichita. I went eight innings in a 4-2 defeat of Alabama's state champs two days before reporting to work for *The News-Gazette* in 1966.

"If I had been any good earlier, those amateur successes might never have happened. I guess I had something to prove to naysayers John Freemuth, Roy Vail and Ecus Vaughn, and to all those collegians that pounded me the first time around."

Royal Giants

Former St. Joseph-Ogden athletes Les Busboom and Deon Flessner were playing sports at the University of Illinois in the late 1960s and hoping to play summer-league baseball at a high level.

Les Busboom

Deon Flessner

"They went out to the countryside of Royal to see where it might be possible to find some land to have a ball diamond," recalled Steve Maddock, who starred for the Royal Giants in the 1970s.

"After being turned down at several possibilities, they came across a cow pasture that had a lot of trees in it."

It happened that the land was owned by Stan Harper, the father of one of Busboom's former high school classmates, Doug Harper. They negotiated a plan to take a portion of the pasture and create a rural baseball diamond.

"In the summer of 1968, they brought in some heavy equipment and started to clear out some trees and build the playing field," Maddock said.

The rent paid by the team to play there offset the profit that would have been made had hay been baled off the land.

"What I think made Harper Park unique was it was the only ballfield in the E.I. that was out in the country," Maddock said. "Being halfway between Royal and Ogden (located southeast of Royal several miles along a black-topped country road) really made it a rural setting. All the trees that were there made it nice to have some shade on those hot Sunday afternoons."

Advertising is visible on the outfield fence at Royal's Harper Park as Brian Remington makes a catch.

Opposing players loved the facility. Jeff Corley started his career at a time when the E.I. featured the area's most unique diamond.

"The thing I remember most about playing," Corley said, "was Harper Park. There was no place like it. The crowds were two or three deep, all the way down the foul lines.

"You could call Harper Park our Field of Dreams."

The sponsoring group went all-out and opened an eating area that Maddock called, "one of the best concession stands in the league. There would be many people who would come after church to have a fish sandwich and eat there. That would get even more people interested in Royal baseball that might not have been before."

As was the custom at E.I. locations when a big showdown was looming, folks made sure to reserve their seating in advance.

"People would bring their trucks and cars out on Saturday morning to line them up along the third base dugout," Maddock said.

The plywood outfield fence was a spot for sponsorships that went to area advertisers. The names would be in full view of players and spectators.

Long before they called Harper Park their home, the team had a ballpark in downtown Royal. After that was no longer available, the Giants played home games in St. Joseph in the early 1960s.

For Maddock, there was a charm about the era when he played and Harper Park was in use.

"The enjoyment that I got out of playing E.I. baseball is all the new friendships that I made that still go on today, not only from teammates, but other players from other teams," he said.

Steve Maddock   Jerry O'Neill

One of the Giants' elite pitchers in the late 1970s and early 1980s was left-hander Jerry O'Neill, who as a 17-year-old in 1970 was a fourth-round draft choice by the Milwaukee Brewers (as well as the first player picked from the state of New York).

O'Neill spent parts of six years in the minor leagues in both the Brewers' and Expos' farm systems. While he didn't make the majors, O'Neill joked that, "I put several players in the big leagues, including Dave Kingman."

He regards Royal's 1977 team, coached by Mitch Frerichs, as one of the most potent he pitched for. The regular lineup featured Les Busboom at first base, Gary Hansgen at second base, Mitch Osterbur at shortstop, Steve Maddock at third base, Stan Cribbett in left field, Rich Connell in center field and Greg Roelfs in right field with Lonnie and Larry Freeman sharing the catching chores.

"I remember being young and feeling invincible, pitching a doubleheader and beating Mike Scholz in the first game going five innings and pitching five innings in the nightcap and beating Bob Harold," O'Neill said. "Marc Frerichs recorded both saves."

The summer of '77 was O'Neill's best. He had a 14-2 record (including postseason games) and posted a league-high 162 strikeouts.

Another personal highlight for the pitcher was the surprise Royal produced for the 1977 regular season champions as they entered tournament play.

"They surprised me by flying my dad from New York to see one of the games," O'Neill said. "That was unbelievable, seeing my dad at the game. The Royal people were super people and really made my family feel welcome. It was a pleasure playing for the community."

O'Neill's father was impressed with the caliber of play.

"My dad followed my career since Little League baseball through professional levels and up to the day he passed away, he thought E.I. baseball was a truly competitive brand of baseball," O'Neill said.

When Royal disbanded for a time, starting after the 1988 season, the baseball field was eventually returned to a farming field.

Ironically, as the 2010 season approaches, one of Royal's on-field coaches will be a Harper descendant, Michael Harper.

Veteran E.I. observers believe Royal participated in one of the top tournament games of all time.

In 1961, in a game hosted by Royal, the Giants and Gifford-Flatville played to a 1-1 deadlock through 12 innings. Tom Fletcher pitched for Royal and Rick Greenfield was on the mound for the Giflats.

The game was replayed the following week and Fletcher pitched Royal to a 5-1 triumph.

Fletcher's father, Glen, had one of the best ironman tournament feats in 1949. At that time, the semifinals and title game were played on the same day. Glen Fletcher pitched Royal to victory in both games, in a tournament hosted by Buckley.

Royal's year-by-year batting leaders, for years it was in the league:

YEAR	NAME	AB	R	H	AVG.
1936	Not available	n/a	n/a	n/a	n/a
1937	Bill Loschen	79	20	31	.392
1938	Louis Meier	45	11	18	.400
1942	Kenneth Roll	50	11	18	.360
1943	Don Cribbett	45	11	17	.378
1944	Not available	n/a	n/a	n/a	n/a
1945	Don Cribbett	52	16	23	.442
1946	Harm Frerichs	43	n/a	17	.395
1947	Bill Felix	60	13	25	.417
1948	Not available	n/a	n/a	n/a	n/a
1949	Rae Blaemire	41	8	17	.415
1950	Bill Parks	62	14	27	.435
1952	Vere Shepherd	19	2	9	.474
1953	Virgil Sweet	25	3	9	.360
1954	Tony Johnson	38	8	18	.474
1956	Herb Osterbur	48	7	14	.292
1957	Hervin Buhr	25	3	10	.400
1958	Derald Meier	44	3	14	.318
1959	Tom Fletcher	54	11	18	.333
1960	Derald Meier	47	9	15	.319
1961	Carl Cooke	42	13	21	.500
1962	Leon Busboom	31	n/a	11	.355
1963	Lou Ryniec	57	16	28	.491

YEAR	NAME	AB	R	H	AVG.
1967	Ron Wrather	26	6	9	.346
1968	Les Busboom	27	8	11	.407
1969	Norbert Franzen	42	9	16	.381
1970	Les Busboom	59	17	23	.390
1971	Stan Cribbett	55	10	25	.455
1972	Les Busboom	94	23	38	.404
1973	Steve Maddock	76	21	25	.329
1974	Ken Fletcher	60	12	18	.300
1975	Rich Connell	55	19	24	.436
1976	Deon Flessner	41	13	14	.341
1977	Mitch Osterbur	85	19	37	.435
1978	Steve Maddock	76	23	33	.434
1979	Not available	n/a	n/a	n/a	n/a
1980	Leroy Kopmann	62	14	23	.371
1981	Bill Bird	51	15	19	.373
1982	Mike Johnson	56	13	24	,429
1983	Les Hoveln	91	25	34	.374
1984	Les Hoveln	86	21	39	.453
1985	Les Hoveln	84	18	35	.417
1986	Jack Peirce	57	9	20	.351
1987	Les Hoveln	87	26	38	.437
1988	Les Hoveln	73	22	32	.438
1994	Robby Auler	27	2	7	.259
2006	Jeff Alexander	58	11	20	.345
2007	Corey Rademacher	47	11	19	.404
2008	Brad McCall	62	11	20	.323
2009	Blake Wolf	64	20	24	.375

Catching Up

Royal's year-by-year pitching leaders:

YEAR	NAME	RECORD	YEAR	NAME	RECORD
1936	Not available	n/a	1969	Les Busboom	6-2
1937	Not available	n/a	1970	Tom Fletcher	5-2
1938	Not available	n/a	1971	Tom Fletcher	4-1
1942	Jay Fletcher	9-1	1972	Tom Fletcher	5-2
1943	Not available	n/a	1973	Stan Osterbur	7-4
1944	Not available	n/a	1974	Nate 'BoBo' Smalls	2-3
1945	Wayne Thornsbrough	6-2	1975	Stan Osterbur	8-1
1946	Not available	n/a	1976	Brian Cork	4-2
1947	Walt Dickerson	7-3	1977	Jerry O'Neill	12-2
1948	Not available	n/a	1978	Jerry O'Neill	11-1
1949	Glen Fletcher	10-2	1979	Not available	n/a
1950	Not available	n/a	1980	Jerry O'Neill	10-3
1952	Jerry McKinney	2-2	1981	Jerry O'Neill	6-2
1953	Jerry McKinney	6-2	1982	Dave McCormick	6-3
1954	Not available	n/a	1983	Jerry O'Neill	5-5
1956	Herb Osterbur	2-1	1984	Jim Maddock	5-4
1957	Herb Osterbur	2-5	1985	Dave McCormick	3-2
1958	Derald Meier	4-7	1986	Duane Johnson	3-6
1959	Derald Meier	4-1	1987	Duane Johnson	9-4
1960	Derald Meier	8-3	1988	Greg 'Chip' Immke	5-9
1961	Tom Fletcher	5-1	1994	Matt Fitzsimmons	2-7
1961	Doug Mills	5-1	2006	Jason Aschenbrenner	3-1
1962	Marty Pattin	6-1	2007	Kyleer Vance	7-2
1963	Gene Creek	4-5	2008	Kyleer Vance	5-2
1967	Vergil Meier	3-2	2009	Trent Duckett	3-5
1968	Les Busboom	7-1			

The 1960s

This was the first year that each team did not supply — and pay for — one of the two umpires in the game. An association was formed with the purpose of providing two impartial umpires for each site. The umpires received $7.50 per game. (In 2010, umpires receive $115 per doubleheader.)

An all-star game, played on Aug. 5 was the first since 1953 and the last until 1972. The North captured a 19-1 victory against the South.

Derald Meier (Royal) and Denny Shelato (Champaign Knights) each pitched three scoreless and hitless innings for the North. Teammate Bill Dexter (Cissna Park) had three hits. Jim Gannaway (Champaign Knights) scored four runs.

Denny Shelato

Starters for the North besides Meier on the mound and Gannaway at third base were Ralph Loschen, Gifford-Flatville, at first base; Bill Weisenbarn, Buckley, at second base; Dick McGee, Royal, at shortstop; Dick Dannehl, Buckley, at catcher; Tony Johnson, Royal, left field; Bob Christensen, Gifford-Flatville, center field; and Ron Franzen, Gifford-Flatville, right field.

Three teams shared the regular season crown. The co-titlists were Buckley, Champaign Eagles and Royal.

1961

There was not a more dominant team during the decade than Royal. The team won or shared five league titles and also captured five tournament championships. In seven of the 10 years, Royal had either a regular season or tourney title. The 1961 regular season crown was the first of five outright titles in a 10-year span.

The most amazing part of Royal's dominance was that it occurred without fielding a team for three successive years (1964-66).

1962

Royal's success was based on its pitching. Future big-leaguer Marty Pattin (6-1) was the catalyst for a squad that won 11 of 14 games but finished seventh in batting (.237 average) in the eight-team league. Derald Meier had a 3-2 record on the mound. Leon Busboom (.355) was the lone Royal hitter among the league's top 10 in batting.

Marty Pattin

Veteran Buckley standout Virgil Scheiwe was forced into retirement as a player after losing an eye in an accident.

1963

At the preseason meeting in April, by a 4-3 vote it was decided that all coaches in the baseline boxes must be in uniform.

Catching Up

Royal, which tied for sixth in the regular season, redeemed itself by winning the tournament crown, 6-2, against the Champaign Dexters in the finals. Carl Cooke, Jerry Fiarito and Hugh Himan all had two hits for Royal.

Pitcher Dick Freehill (a sophomore at the University of Illinois) fired a four-hitter and had a 2-0 lead before he took the mound in the bottom of the first inning at Gifford on Aug. 25.

For three postseason games, Royal had the top three hitters: Cooke (.556), Fiarito (.538) and Himan (.500).

Royal's tournament roster: Leon Busboom, Terry Casper, Carl Cooke, Gene Creek, Jerry Fiarito, Jeff Ferguson, Tom Fletcher, Dick Freehill, Hugh Himan, William Myers, Lowell Osterbur, Wayne Osterbur, Jim Reed, Joe Rosado, Lou Ryniec and Carl Thompson. Harm W. Frerichs and Ryniec were the team's managers.

During the regular season, the eight-team league was controlled by the three Champaign entries: the Dexters were first (11-2), followed by the Knights (9-4) and then the Eagles (8-6).

Gene Creek

1963 All-Stars:

Catcher, Joe Dwyer, Buckley
First base, Tom Fletcher, Royal
Second base, Rochell Broome, Champaign Eagles
Shortstop, Lou Ryniec, Royal
Third base, Dick Newell, Champaign Knights
Left field, Bill Weisenbarn, Buckley
Center field, Al Bousquet, Chanute
Right field, John Cooper, Champaign Eagles
Pitcher, Joe Hamende, Champaign Dexters
Utility, (tie) Butch Kemmer, Buckley, and Roy Radmaker, Champaign Knights

1964

The Champaign Dexters beat St. Joseph 6-2 in the tournament title game on Aug. 30 in Buckley.

Fred Schooley had two hits and three RBI for the Dexters. Lee Schinker pitched a complete-game four-hitter. The left-hander struck out 10 while outpitching Vergil Meier.

The Dexters' tournament roster: Dave Crouse, Jerry Fiarito, Jeff Ferguson, Jerry Hamende, Charles Hursey, Fred Klemm, Ernie Kumerow, Bill Martin, Bob Michaletti, Bob Rasmussen, Lou Ryniec, Jim Sanders, Lee Schinker, Fred Schooley, Doug Smith, Hal Weisenbarn and Ernie Westfield.

The regular season home run champion, Lou Ryniec, from the Champaign Eagles, was the first person to reach double figures for the season. He swatted 10 round-trippers.

Charles Hursey

Managers:

Buckley, Bob Weisenbarn
Champaign Eagles, Wardell Jackson

Chanute, Daniel Ferguson Jr., and Sgt. Willie Harris
Gifford-Flatville, Harm Frerichs and Ralph Loschen
Mayor Dexter's, Bob Leach and Ray Sanders
St. Joseph, Al Hill and Derald Meier
Commissioners:
Rae Blaemire, President
Bill Burrows, Secretary-treasurer
Al Ellsworth
E.W. Hesse
Al Nelson

1965

A first-time entry, Danville, captured the regular season crown with a 12-3 record, which was one game in front of runner-up Gifford-Flatville. Those teams were deadlocked entering the Aug. 22 season-ender against each other.

Guy Corey homered and led Danville to a 4-3 triumph. Left-hander Parker Eaton held the Giflats to six hits. Danville's 13-hit attack was led by Max Crotser and Dean Little, with three hits each. Danville's coaches were Ross Harvey and Charles Goble.

1966

1966 All-Stars:
Catcher, Barry Moore, Champaign Eagles
First base, Norlyn Loschen, Gifford-Flatville
Second base, Val Bush, Rantoul
Shortstop, Butch Kemmer, Buckley
Third base, Deon Flessner, St. Joseph
Outfield, Ron Franzen, Rantoul
Outfield, Gordie Hull, Buckley
Outfield, Ernie Westfield, Champaign Eagles
Pitcher, Terry Thomas, Champaign Eagles

Ron   Terry
Franzen   Thomas

1967

In its first year back in the league, Royal struggled throughout the regular season (team batting average of .200) and finished with a sub-.500 record (7-8). The Giants turned it on at tournament time, securing a championship and starting a still-unmatched streak of four consecutive postseason titles. Ron Wrather (.346) was the only squad member to finish among the top 15 in batting. Five pitchers had decisions, with Vergil Meier (3-2) heading the mound corps.

In the tournament, Royal opened with a 4-0 win against the Champaign Eagles before clubbing runner-up Buckley 15-5 in the semifinals. In the title game, the Giants edged a Tuscola opponent which had blanked two foes to reach the finals, 8-7.

Batting champion Louie Krumwiede, from Buckley, became the sixth player to also win the home run title in the same season. Entering the 75th E.I. season, this accomplishment has occurred 14 times.

Those who have done it:

Catching Up

YEAR	PLAYER, TEAM
1948	Eldred 'Bumps' Hadley, Thomasboro
1949	Bud Bitter, Sidney
1952	Bob Ems, Thomasboro
1955	Rocky Raklovits, Champaign Knights
1963	Lou Ryniec, Royal
1967	Louie Krumwiede, Buckley
1971	Bill Gillispie, Rantoul
1972	Bill Gillispie, Rantoul
1982	Bill Elliott, Thomasboro
1992	Andy Small, Thomasboro
1994	Ken Crawford, Thomasboro
1995	Ken Crawford, Thomasboro
2001	Jake Krause, Buckley
2007	Luke Humphrey, Paxton

Andy Small

1968

Gifford did not field a team in 1968, but its ball diamond did not go unused. Rantoul played its home games in Gifford.

E.I. commissioner John Franzen commented in an April 23 newspaper article about the reasons for Gifford's departure.

"There are guys around there that want to play ball," Franzen said, "but nobody wants to manage."

Royal's country Harper Park made its debut this season. In the tournament title game played Sept. 2, 1968 on the new field, Royal needed 10 innings to subdue Buckley, 7-6. Lowell Osterbur tripled in the 10th and scored the decisive run on a passed ball. Les Busboom struck out 10 and pitched a complete game for the win.

Royal scored a run in the bottom of the ninth to create a 6-6 tie and force extra innings. The equalizer was scored by Les Busboom on Bob Shapland's infield hit.

For the game, Mike Rubenacher and Ron Wrather each had two hits for the Giants. Mick Larson, who suffered the loss for Buckley, was 4 for 5. Teammate Butch Kemmer had two doubles and Louie Krumwiede scored two runs.

Les Busboom, left, and Ron Wrather

1969

Royal recorded the first of two consecutive championship-game shutouts against Rantoul, posting a 1-0 triumph in the finals on Aug. 22 at Royal. Tom Fletcher outdueled Denny Shelato in a game where each hurler issued just one walk in nine innings. Fletcher fanned 14 and twirled a five-hitter.

All of the hits he allowed came in the first two innings. He settled down and retired the last 16 batters he faced.

The lone Royal run was scored in the sixth inning by Gary Wrather, who was 2 for-2. He doubled, took third on a fly ball by Mitch Osterbur, and scored on a passed ball with Bob Shapland at-bat. Shapland then stroked a single.

Osterbur and Wrather were the game's only players with more than one hit.

Royal's starting lineup in the title game:

Catcher, Norbert Franzen
First base, Mitch Frerichs
Second base, Bob Shapland
Shortstop, Mitch Osterbur
Third base, Mike Rubenacher
Left field, Deon Flessner
Center field, Gary Wrather
Right field, Terry White
Pitcher, Tom Fletcher
Coach, Don Cribbett

Stars of the 1960s

Tom Fletcher

Tom Fletcher's E.I. debut occurred the summer before his junior year at Oakwood High School.

"I was 15 and in my first game (in 1958), I pitched against the (Champaign) Eagles and Dubois McCullough (who later pitched in the New York Mets organization) and I got beat," he recalled.

Eight months after he pitched in his first — and only — major league baseball game, 20-year-old Tom Fletcher received special permission from the Illinois High School Association to play for the Royal Giants.

An arm ailment prevented Fletcher from pitching professionally in 1963, so he returned home for his rehab and to take summer classes at Eastern Illinois University. Royal coaches Harm W. Frerichs and Don Cribbett wanted to put Fletcher in the lineup as a position player.

The appeal to the IHSA was deemed necessary so teenaged players on the team would not jeopardize their scholastic eligibility.

"They did it to be on the safe side," Fletcher said.

In his opinion, the fuss was unnecessary.

"I wasn't under contract (with the Detroit Tigers)," he said. "I went on the voluntary retired list, which kept me off waivers."

On May 6, 1963, the IHSA ruled in Royal's favor.

Albert Willis, the IHSA's executive secretary, issued a written statement which read: "I wish to advise you that if Tom does not accept pay for playing

Wayne Osterbur, left, and Tom Fletcher

in league games, I do not believe that high school boys would make themselves ineligible by playing with or against him.

"While IHSA rules provide that high school boys may not play on teams on which there are paid players, the Board of Directors of the Association have always interpreted this to mean that the player must not receive pay for playing in the specific games in which high school boys are involved."

Fletcher not only played, he excelled.

As a first baseman, he delivered 11 hits in 31 at-bats (.355 batting average) after his activation and was chosen as the E.I.'s All-Star first baseman for a season when the Giants captured the tournament championship.

He appreciated the opportunity to stay active in baseball.

"I was getting ready to go to the Florida Instructional League in September," Fletcher said.

He spent five more seasons in the minors — including three in AAA — but was never called back up by the parent team despite a career 2.98 earned run average covering 662 career minor league innings (167 of which were at the AAA level).

Fletcher, a 6-foot left-hander, made his major league debut 18 days before the 1962 season ended, joining a team that featured Norm Cash and Al Kaline. He worked two innings against the Boston Red Sox.

During a portion of the time he was away from the E.I., a pitcher from Eastern Illinois University joined Royal's Giants. Marty Pattin later played in the major leagues. Though Tom Fletcher and Pattin were never teammates, they had a memorable game together.

"We pitched against each other in the Pacific Coast League (AAA) when he was with the Angels and I was with the Cubs," Fletcher said.

Fletcher returned home in 1969 and pitched five more seasons for Royal, compiling a cumulative 18-6 record before retiring following the '73 campaign.

Ernie Westfield

Ernie Westfield celebrated his 70th birthday in 2009. His playing days are behind him, but his association with the game remains as strong as ever.

"I'm trying to encourage kids to come back to baseball," Westfield said.

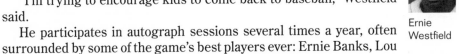
Ernie Westfield

He participates in autograph sessions several times a year, often surrounded by some of the game's best players ever: Ernie Banks, Lou Brock, Rickey Henderson, Stan Musial and Billy Williams.

Through no fault of his own, Westfield does not have the same name recognition nationally. As a 20-year-old, he was signed to play for the Birmingham Black Barons, an independent team at one time associated with the Negro American League, which was owned by Wardell Jackson, a prominent figure in Champaign-Urbana in the 1960s and 1970s.. He reported that he signed for a $300 bonus and a monthly salary of $175.

The year was 1959.

A year later, he was the starting pitcher in the East-West All-Star Game at Chicago's Comiskey Park. The 6-foot-3, 160-pounder was described in accounts of the game as "a skinny, flamethrowing 21-year-old."

Westfield's break came when he was asked to pitch against the touring Black Barons when they played in his native Tennessee.

"I beat them," Westfield said.

Jackson also owned the Philadelphia Stars and, Westfield said, the teams were "based out of here (Champaign). We stayed at the Inman Hotel."

Westfield and right-hander Dubois McCullough were the pitching aces for the Black Barons. They relocated to the Champaign-Urbana communities and played for various E.I. teams in which Jackson was associated, notably the Champaign Eagles.

"My best memory," Westfield said, "was pitching against Tom Fletcher the year he was 10-0 and an All-American at the UI. Lee (Eilbracht, Illini coach) allowed him to leave and pitch against me with the Eagles.

Catching Up

"The score was 0-0 after six innings when Lou Ryniec hit a home run off of me."

For Jackson's faults, Westfield credits him for opening up baseball opportunities for dozens of players. He had teams in the E.I. League for 17 seasons.

"If not for Wardell, there would not have been any baseball in the black community," Westfield said. "He was a gambler and a very colorful character, but he loved the game of baseball and was involved in baseball for years."

Dubois McCullough eventually signed a professional contract with the New York Mets organization, but the 23-year-old was shot to death in Urbana on Christmas Day 1961, in the offseason following his first year in the pros. McCullough, under minor league contract with the Mets (who made their National League debut in 1962), had a 9-3 record in 1961 while pitching for a Class D affiliate in Lexington, N.C. He tied for the team lead in victories and started 10 of the 18 games in which he appeared.

"He threw a low fastball, and I couldn't understand how he kept it so low," Westfield said.

In 1960, his fourth summer in the E.I., McCullough starred for the Champaign Eagles and compiled a 9-2 record for a squad which shared the regular season title and won the tournament championship. He was killed by a shotgun he had owned until about a month before his death, when he sold it to his second cousin, Sanders Hillsman, for $7.

Four months after the shooting, Hillsman was acquitted when a judge ruled he was in defense of his habitation and thus wasn't guilty of either murder or manslaughter.

McCullough, who grew up in Trezevant, Tenn., also pitched for the Danville Boosters and the Champaign Colts. In three-plus seasons with Jackson's E.I. Eagles, his overall record was 26-7.

Among the other noteworthy E.I. players Westfield played with — or against — were Rochell Broome, Les Busboom, Parker Eaton, Deon Flessner, Charles Hursey, Marty Pattin, George Peterson, Mike Peterson, Roy Radmaker, Bob Rasmussen, Fred Schooley, Denny Shelato and Nate 'BoBo' Smalls as well as the pitcher he said "gave me the most trouble: Mike Scholz."

He remembers Pattin, who eventually reached the major leagues as someone who "threw exceptionally hard," and Ivesdale native Radmaker as "one of the best hitters out of the E.I. League."

Westfield played on and off in the E.I. League from 1961 to 1975. "I see a lot of the people I played in the E.I. and there's nothing but good memories," said Westfield, who now is CEO of ELW Enterprises, which sells Negro League memorabilia.

In 1963 and 1964, the Champaign Dexters, featuring left-handed pitcher Lee Schinker, along with team leaders Westfield and Ryniec, won back-to-back E.I. crowns. Other prominent squad members for a team coached by Bob Leach (who disbanded the team in 1969 because he could no longer afford it) were Hursey, Schooley, Rasmussen, Joe Hamende, Fred Klemm, Jim Sanders, L.C. Sweet, Frank Strainis and Phil Summers.

Bill Gillispie

He won batting championships three of the four years he played in the E.I. League, but Chanute airman Bill Gillispie Jr. never received credit for his accomplishments.

In every newspaper article published during his years in Rantoul (1969-72), the recognition was attributed to Bill Gillespie. The player never complained about the misspelling.

Gillispie had made a name for himself in baseball prior to joining the Air Force as a 19-year-old and serving as a medic.

In 1964, he was part of the integration of the Gastonia (N.C.) American Legion baseball team. He and center fielder Elmore Hill were described in a newspaper article as the first "two Negro athletes in North Carolina on an American Legion baseball team."

Two years later, as a 17-year-old, Gillispie was the team's top batter (.419). When he relocated to central Illinois, Gillispie was hoping to continue in baseball.

"I thought maybe the Air Force would have a team," he said. "I figured I'd find somewhere to play ball."

Champaign Eagles standouts, from left, Willie McCullum, Ernie Westfield and Bill Gillispie

Through another airman, Al Byrd, Gillispie was introduced to Wardell Jackson, the Champaign tavern owner who had an E.I. team, the Champaign Eagles. Gillispie played a year for the Eagles before switching to the Rantoul team "because it was closer."

His first E.I. batting title came in 1969, when he hit .510 (28 for 55) for the Eagles. A year later, he ended 21st (.281) before he closed his career with back-to-back titles at Rantoul (.500 in 1971, 31 for 62, and .483 in 1972, 43 for 89).

His cumulative four-year batting average (.444) earned him a spot on the all-time E.I. All-Star team, chosen by *The News-Gazette* in 2009.

As one might suspect, there were few pitchers who routinely gave Gillispie trouble.

"I didn't have too much problem with too many of them," he said.

The left-handed batter recalls two hurlers — both left-handers — who were his biggest nemesis.

"Tom Fletcher (Royal) was tough on me from time to time, but I was tough on him from time to time," Gillispie said. "He was throwing in the 80s to 90s (mph).

Rodell Gerdes (Paxton) was another one. He couldn't break a window pane, but he gave me trouble with his off-speed stuff."

Gerdes compiled a 10-2 record in 1972, the same year Fletcher was 5-2 and one of the league leaders in strikeouts (55).

Gillispie recalls the lone season he didn't hit at least .483 with a touch of irony.

"The year I hit .281, I hit the ball harder than all the years I won batting titles," Gillispie said. "It was just right at someone."

One of Gillispie's most memorable performances occurred on Aug. 8, 1971, at Royal. Entering the final game of the regular season, Rantoul's record was 11-4. The Merchants were playing a Royal team that was 10-5 and could tie for the league crown with a victory.

Fletcher, 4-0 for the season, was Royal's pitcher. He was pitted against Roy Radmaker.

Fletcher struck out 18 in the nine-inning contest, but cleanup batter Gillispie was 5 for 5 and the hero in Rantoul's 10-8 triumph.

He slugged a two-out, two-strike pitch over the 365-foot sign in right-center field for a home run that lifted the Merchants into a 9-8 lead. His blast drove in Ron Ingrum, who had walked.

Three weeks later, the same teams played in the E.I. Tournament championship game at Gifford on Aug. 29. Fletcher was opposed by Rantoul's Denny Shelato. Del Ryan and Gillispie drew walks in the top of the first inning and center fielder Ron Franzen drilled a three-run homer that started Rantoul on its way to a 15-1 triumph. Shelato pitched a five-hitter and walked no one. Fletcher fanned four in four innings but was touched for eight hits.

Gillispie's Air Force stint was finished nearly two months prior to the conclusion of the 1972 E.I. season, but he stayed with his team. His impact was so strong that E.I. managers for nearly two decades continued to list Gillispie on their rosters in hopes of using him if he returned.

Ironically, he has returned dozens of times. While working part time at Urbana's Mercy Hospital as an orderly he became friends with Edna Thorp. They eventually married and return annually to visit family.

"I used to come every November to go pheasant hunting," said Gillispie, who continued to play semi-professional baseball in North Carolina until he was 45.

The urge still hadn't left him and earlier this decade he joined a 30-and-over league in Charlotte.

"I was the oldest guy on the team (56 in 2004)," he said. "By the time I got my timing down, the season was about half over, but I finished up with a decent average."

After undergoing open heart surgery in 2007, Gillispie officially retired as a competitive player.

He remembers the comments he heard after leaving the Eagles to play for Rantoul.

"People used to accuse Rantoul of paying me," he said. "They never gave me no money to play, but I got plenty of beer to drink."

He has fond memories of his career in the league.

"The E.I. had great ballplayers," he said. "Guys who could flat-out play. It was fun."

Rochell Broome

Chuck Robinson Sr., from Danville, wrote a remembrance for *The News-Gazette* about Rochell Broome, who died in 2009. Robinson wrote:

"I remember Rochell Broome as a flamboyant-type ballplayer. He had a certain swagger and way that he carried himself. He wasn't your typical A-B-C type of guy who just did the ordinary. To me, he is a guy who stood out in the crowd as far as a ballplayer.

"He was a shortstop who had good range, a strong arm, soft hands and great baseball savvy. He was probably one of the better infielders that I have seen on the local level in turning the double play. He and second baseman Toby Pritchett were an exceptional combination. What stood out so much was their ability to flip the ball underhand, which you don't see a lot today. His nickname (Sweeper) was probably from his fielding ability and meant he could pick up most things that came his way.

"He was a good hitter, a lefty with a sweet, fluid swing. He was a clutch hitter and a good RBI man. With the game on the line, he is the one I'd want to see at the plate, or on the other side of the ball, defensively I'd like to see the ball hit to him to make the final out. He was the go-to man.

"I had the pleasure of playing with him a few times and, as a catcher, I had confidence when you throw the ball, whether it was a good or bad throw, they (Broome or Pritchett) could usually come up with it.

"He played in the Negro American League (for the Kansas City Monarchs) and for the Champaign Eagles. Back then, guys had a great passion for the game and were easy to talk to. They would take younger guys under their wing to help develop their skills. I discussed baseball several times with Rochell. He had a lot to offer. We would share our philosophies and different approaches to the game. After Rochell left the game as a player, he went on to coach at the U of I. He was a very personable guy, a caring person who wanted to see the best for others. He came to me with ideas to enhance my business (Kag's BBQ)."

Broome was the E.I.'s 1963 all-star second baseman and a two-time home run champion.

The 1970s

No other decade embodies the term "glory years" as much as the end of this decade. Starting in 1977 and continuing for three seasons, the E.I. had its largest number of participants.

The 14 teams were divided into two seven-team divisions.

Earlier in the decade, the E.I. had its first team post a 20-win season, Rantoul surpassing that previously unreachable barrier during a 21-9 campaign in 1972. That same summer, Paxton won 20 of 30 games.

Mike Scholz

The 1970s also produced what is considered the greatest league game ever played. The 1974 tournament championship game between Gifford-Flatville and Rantoul required 15 innings before the Giflats and "Iron" Mike Scholz — who pitched every inning of the contest — secured a 1-0 victory.

Even prior to the championship encounter, played in Gifford on Aug. 25, the 1974 season had left an indelible impression on E.I. historians. It was the first time in the league's existence that two teams tied for first, two tied for third and two tied for fifth.

Fittingly, Gifford-Flatville and Rantoul had shared the No. 1 spot, compiling 16-4 records. Sharing third place, with 13-7 marks, were Buckley and Paxton. The fifth-place finishers, Royal and Tuscola, concluded the regular season with 8-10 slates.

To reach the tourney finale, Rantoul used home runs by Terry Green and Vic Boblett to overpower Buckley 10-4 in one semifinal game. Cleanup batter Norlyn Loschen's two doubles, a single and a home run helped the Giflats top Paxton 12-6 in the other semifinal.

The championship showdown served as a rematch of the season openers. On May 26, Rantoul swept the Giflats 2-0 and 7-6. Entering the tournament finale, however, Gifford-Flatville was carrying a 12-game winning streak.

Steve Ward, who'd fired a three-hit shutout in the regular season game, was given the game ball by manager Hans Flessner for the tournament finale. His mound adversary was another right-hander, Mike Scholz, who'd won 11 games in succession after losing to Rantoul on a four-hitter.

Both Ward, a Champaign native, and Scholz, a Decatur native, were up to the challenge on an ideal day for the championship. After 14 innings, with dusk approaching, the umpires convened and said Inning No. 15 would be the day's final one. Both starting pitchers were still in the game and would finish with complete-game eight-hitters.

The Giflats managed a run in the top of the 15th without a ball being hit in fair territory. Left fielder Frank Abney, the No. 6 batter in the lineup for G-F co-coaches Dick Franzen and Ralph Loschen, struck out to start the inning. Right fielder Dwayne Gossett was hit by a pitch, and *News-Gazette* sports writer E.W.

Hesse wrote, "proceeded to surprise Rantoul by stealing second, and a moment later charged to third when Ward, attempting a pickoff, threw past second into center field."

That brought up Phil Rogers, whose foul ball near the right field fence was chased down by Rantoul first baseman Steve Engstrom for the second out. Gossett tagged up after the catch and scored the decisive run.

Scholz, who struck out at least one batter in every inning, completed his record 27-strikeout performance and secured Gifford-Flatville's ninth tournament crown. He ended the season with a 12-1 record. His catcher for the game was his brother, Pat Scholz. Both Mike and Pat Scholz had two hits apiece against Ward, who fanned 11. Abney had three hits, including the only extra-base hit (a double).

Rantoul's leadoff batter, Del Ryan, had three of his team's hits. Ward, who ended the year with a 10-3 record, added two hits.

That same day, a preliminary third-place game was played between the teams which had tied for third in the regular season. Kevin Sprau and Mark Schultz teamed up on a three-hit, 15-strikeout performance as Buckley edged Paxton 3-2. The Dutch Masters snapped a 2-2 tie in the fourth inning when Greg Halm's sacrifice fly drove in Rick Hull with the decisive run.

1970

1970 All-Stars:
    Catcher, Bill Gillispie, Rantoul
    First base, (tie) Mitch Frerichs, Royal,
        and John Gordon, Champaign Eagles
    Second base, Willie Southall, Champaign
        Eagles
    Shortstop, Mitch Osterbur, Royal
    Third base, Denny Shelato, Rantoul
    Outfield, Les Busboom, Royal
    Outfield, Larry Bundy, Gifford-Flatville
    Outfield, Gordie Hull, Buckley
    Pitcher, Dan Lathrop, Rantoul

Mitch Frerichs   John Gordon   Willie Southall

1971

The league had its fewest number of teams to date (five) in 1971 but quickly recovered. In 1977, 1978 and 1979, the league had ballooned to 14 teams divided into two divisions.

Rantoul's Bill Gillispie clinched the batting title on the final day of the regular season, Aug. 8. He went 5 for 5 in a 10-8 win against Royal. His closest pursuer was on the other side of the field. Royal's Stan Cribbett went 2 for 5. Gillispie ended the summer with a .500 average (31 for 62) and Cribbett came in at .455 (25 for 55). Gillispie's performance came on a day when Royal's Tom Fletcher struck out 18 batters in a nine-inning game.

Tom Fletcher   Ivan 'Bud' Eichelberger

1971 managers:
    Buckley, Joe Dwyer
    Gifford-Flatville, Dick Franzen and Ralph Loschen
    Paxton, Carl Hudson Jr., and Ivan 'Bud' Eichelberger
    Rantoul, Phil Quinlan
    Royal, Wayne Osterbur
Commissioners:
    Al Ellsworth, President
    E.W. Hesse
    Lawrence 'Boots' Maier
    Virgil Scheiwe
    John Radmaker

The season was supposed to be a historical one. Commissioners voted to play weekly doubleheaders of seven innings for the first time, abandoning a system of one nine-inning game that had been in place since the league was formed.

This decision was made, over the objections of Buckley's Virgil Scheiwe, when it appeared that Ivesdale would rejoin, creating a six-team league. When Ivesdale made a late decision to pull out, the doubleheader proposition was delayed one year.

Scheiwe was quoted in an April 21 edition of *The News-Gazette* saying, "It will be hard to sell Buckley fans on the idea that a baseball game should be anything but nine innings long."

What happened for the first time this season was a double-elimination setup in the tournament. Rantoul emerged victorious, throttling Royal 15-1 in the title game at Gifford on Aug. 29.

Denny Shelato pitched a nine-inning five-hitter, walked no one and struck out two as the Merchants ended the summer with a 15-4 overall record. He was backed by a 19-hit attack, including three hits each from Gary Buhr, Ron Franzen, Bill Gillispie and Greg McKaufsky. Franzen and Del Ryan each homered.

1972

An All-Star Game was revived following an absence of 12 years. Paxton's Rodell Gerdes, Rantoul's Dan Lathrop and Rantoul's Denny Shelato teamed up for a shutout as the North posted a 6-0 victory. Paxton's Jim Fox had a single and a triple and drove in three runs. Gerdes was the winning pitcher.

In conjunction with the revived All-Star Game was the first Old-Timers Game (July 26 at Buckley), which attracted 38 former stars, including former batting champions Don Cribbett (Royal, 1945) and Carl Wolf (Buckley, 1947) as well as standout pitchers Ehm Franzen (Flatville) and Virgil Scheiwe (Buckley).

The concept was so successful it was continued two more years but then was abandoned after the 1974 game when just 20 former players showed up. When

Rantoul pitchers Denny Shelato, left, and Dan Lathrop

the next Old-Timers Game was held, in 1982, a total of 68 former players participated.

Royal won this season's tournament championship, overpowering Paxton 10-6 in the latest title game in E.I. history. The game, played in Royal, was played on Oct. 1. Left-hander Stan Osterbur was staked to a 7-0 lead — thanks in part to home runs by Ken Fletcher and Deon Flessner — and the Giants made the margin hold up.

Mick Larson

The first year for weekly doubleheaders also marked the first time a team produced a 20-win season. Rantoul was 21-9.

The league's top catcher was Buckley's Mick Larson, who one year earlier was the league's top pitcher.

1973

Nate 'BoBo' Smalls, who pitched for the barnstorming Indianapolis Clowns early in the summer — including a game at Buckley — joined Royal and made an immediate impact. He won his first three decisions, including a 15-strikeout performamce in a 4-1 victory against Gifford-Flatville and a nine-strikeout effort in a 6-1 triumph against Rantoul. His first loss was in a 5-0 decision against Thomasboro when Terry Krueger fired a two-hitter.

Nate 'BoBo' Smalls

Smalls was the starter and pitched five innings in the tournament title game, which Royal won 11-5 against Buckley on Sept. 30, in Buckley. Reliever Tom Fletcher fanned eight in four innings of relief and earned the win. Fletcher had played in only four regular season games. Steve Maddock and Stan Cribbett — the first two batters in coach Herb Osterbur's lineup — each had three hits for the Giants.

1973 managers:
    Buckley, Wes Hethke
    Gibson City, Eldon Christensen
    Gifford-Flatville, Dick Franzen and Ralph Loschen
    Paxton, Dan Phillips
    Rantoul, Hans Flessner
    Royal, Herb Osterbur
    Thomasboro, Leon Ehmen
    Tuscola, Jim Hardesty
Commissioners:
    Al Ellsworth, President
    Glen Fletcher
    E.W. Hesse
    Lawrence 'Boots' Maier
    John Radmaker

1974

Gifford-Flatville's Mike Scholz (10-1 record with 120 strikeouts in 75 $^2/_3$ innings, headlined the nine-player All-Star team.

The other first-teamers: Tuscola catcher Joe Lange (.333 average), Giflat first baseman Norlyn Loschen (.339), Buckley second baseman Tom Posey (.500),

Giflat shortstop Jan South (.414), Farmer City-Mansfield third baseman Jim Hays (.390), Rantoul left fielder Greg Garland (.387), Rantoul center fielder Del Ryan (.348) and Royal right fielder Ken Fletcher (.366).

The league batting average that summer was .259.

Neither Paxton nor Thomasboro had a home field in its community. Paxton played its home games in Rantoul and T'boro shared Royal's field.

1975

The admission price for this season's tournament championship game was $1.50. Also, a record number of six commissioners were seated. Joining league president Al Ellsworth were holdovers Lawrence 'Boots' Maier, John Radmaker and E.W. Hesse along with newcomers Ehm Franzen and Don Cribbett.

A Champaign entry returned for the first time in five years. The team, under the direction of player-manager Glenn Karr, lost its first game on May 18 to Thomasboro 5-1 but rebounded with a flourish. Steve Wertz, who played third base in the opener, took the mound in Game 2 and fired a no-hitter as Champaign prevailed 4-1 to secure a split. Terry Shoemaker and Bill Uden had key run-scoring hits to support the pitching of Wertz, who fanned eight but walked six.

Steve Wertz

Gifford-Flatville turned on the power for its May 26 sweep of Farmer City-Mansfield in Mansfield. The Giflats slugged nine home runs before completing the 10-1 and 14-6 triumphs. Norlyn Loschen socked four homers. Teammate Jan South hit two.

Because the high school season was still ongoing, a temporary snow fence was in place, 300 feet down the lines and 340 to straightaway center.

The onslaught continued when FC-M hosted its second twinbill. After four games at the field, 20 total home runs had been hit. By comparison, 40 other league games had produced only an additional 13 homers.

The fence, however, had little benefit for the home team, managed by Carlos Burton. The team was 0-4 in its first four home games.

Loschen, incidentally, won the home run title. His final total was four, all of which were swatted on the same day.

The regular season title was settled on the last day, Aug. 3. Rantoul swept Buckley on the road behind the pitching of Kevin Sprau (7-2) and Dan Lathrop (8-0) to finish the season with a 17-3 record. Lathrop's win was the 71st of his career.

Pitching and defense carried Rantoul throughout the summer. In 20 games, the team allowed 29 runs.

Dan Lathrop

Runner-up Royal won its final doubleheader against visiting Thomasboro behind the pitching of Mike Ellsworth (6-3) and Stan Osterbur (8-1) to end with a 16-4 season record.

The top batter for the tournament was Buckley's Tom Posey. He was 9 for 15, a .600 batting average. Gifford-Flatville's Mike Scholz was the top postseason hurler, striking out 28 while going 3-0 in tournament action.

Scholz was the winner in a 9-7 title-game decision against Buckley in Buckley. Pat Scholz and Frank Abney each had three hits for the Giflats. Stan Feller had three of Buckley's 11 hits.

1975 All-Stars:

     Catcher, Lonnie Freeman, Royal

     First base, Norlyn Loschen, Gifford-Flatville

     Second base, Dave Reel, Mattoon

     Shortstop, Jon Siron, Gifford-Flatville

     Third base, Tom Posey, Buckley

     Outfield, Rich Connell, Royal

     Outfield, Greg Garland, Rantoul

     Outfield, Stan Feller, Buckley

     Designated hitter, Lou Due, Royal

     Pitchers, (tie) Dan Lathrop, Rantoul; Mike Scholz, Gifford-Flatville, an Kevin Sprau, Rantoul

1976

The batting champion wasn't determined until Aug. 15, the date for the regular season finales. Buckley's Tom Posey was 1 for 4, ending at .480 (36 for 75) while runner-up Jeff Corley, from Thomasboro, was 1 for 2 and came in at .473 (35 for 74). Posey was also the 1974 batting champion (.500).

Tom
Posey

The Giflats' Mike Scholz opened the 1976 season by no-hitting Farmer City-Mansfield 2-0 on May 16. His single drove in Renard Danenhower with the team's first run.

Farmer City-Mansfield, held to three hits in the nightcap, salvaged a 3-2 win thanks to the heroics of Tom Bernett. His two-run triple accounted for the team's first runs in the opening inning. Bernett doubled in the ninth and advanced twice on wild pitches.

Bernett had an impressive game at Tolono on July 18. In the second game of a doubleheader, won by Farmer City-Mansfield 12-4, he hit for the cycle and knocked in nine runs. Bernett terrorized E.I. pitchers that summer. Sixteen of his first 23 hits were for extra bases. One of his prodigious home runs prompted Rantoul manager Jack Herbert to measure the distance. Herbert said the blast traveled 483 feet. Ironically, the left-handed hitting Bernett had hit the home run against a fellow left-hander, Mahomet's Calvin Pollard, in a tournament game at the Knights of Columbus field in Rantoul.

Scholz, meanwhile, followed his early no-hitter with back-to-back one-hitters and then a two-hitter. In his first 29 innings of the season, he did not yield a run. The wrapup to the season produced another series of outstanding efforts from the league's premier teams. The semifinalists were Gifford-Flatville (20-3), Buckley (17-6), Thomasboro (17-6) and Rantoul (15-8). Each squad was anchored by pitchers who produced dominant seasons. Mike Scholz was 12-0 for the Giflats, Buckley ace Steve Stahlman was 10-2, T'boro's John Harshbarger was 8-2 and Rantoul's Kevin Sprau was 7-2.

Though three of the Dutch Masters' losses had been administered by the Giflats, Buckley gained its revenge in the finale, posting a 9-5 win that ended G-F's 10-game winning streak.

Steve
Stahlman

"I had a few good years and one great year during the seasons I played," said Stahlman, the title-game winner thanks to three hitless innings of sterling relief from Mark Schultz.

Preparation was the key, Stahlman said.

"We drove to Danville every Wednesday to play in a league to keep our game sharp," Stahlman said. "We had a great run."

Batting champion Tom Posey (.480 average) spearheaded the potent offensive attack for coach Virgil Scheiwe's Buckley squad,which also got major contributions from Gordie Hull (.441).

The effort is what still remains vivid for Stahlman.

"Stu Trask ran through our outfield wall," he recalled.

1977

The storied career of Rantoul right-handed Dan Lathrop came to a disappointing conclusion on July 1. Married and tired of making the weekly commute from Charleston, he asked for a transfer to nearby Mattoon, which had joined the league two years earlier. He was granted a verbal release, but the paperwork was not filed with the Board of Commissioners before he pitched two innings of relief for Mattoon on June 26 and hit a homer in a 14-1 win. The game was forfeited and the transfer was not allowed, though the 30-year-old Lathrop was told he could continue to play for Rantoul. Instead, however, he retired, ending his 12-year career with 77 victories. Quoted in a June 26, 1982 story, the 6-foot-3 Lathrop told *The News-Gazette,* "I was generally disgusted with the way things went in 1977. I have some great memories, but it was a bittersweet end."

1977 All-Stars:

Dan Lathrop   Renard Danenhower

    Catcher, Lonnie Freeman, Royal
    First base, Norlyn Loschen, Gifford-Flatville
    Second base, David Hays, Monticello
    Shortstop, Gary Buhr, Rantoul
    Third base, Renard Danenhower, Gifford-Flatville
    Outfield, Mike Beaird, Mattoon
    Outfield, Glen Mitchell, Rantoul
    Outfield, Jan South, Gifford-Flatville
    Pitcher, Mike Scholz, Gifford-Flatville

1978

Mike Scholz pitched Gifford-Flatville to the tournament championship crown, blanking Mattoon and John Widdersheim 2-0. A few weeks earlier, to determine the regular season titlist, South Division champion Mattoon bested North Division champion Gifford-Flatville 7-3.

This year stands above all others for the most 20-win teams in a season (four). Mattoon was 22-6. In the North, Royal was 22-6, Gifford-Flatville was 21-5 and Buckley 20-8.

Royal and the Giflats played in a controversial regular season ending doubleheader in Royal. The Giflats won the opener 9-7 to improve to 20-5. The loss dropped Royal's mark to 22-5.

In Game 2 G-F led 2-0 in the bottom of the sixth in when the Giants started their comeback. Stan Cribbett walked and Mitch Osterbur singled, putting the tying runs on base as batting champion Steve Maddock strode to the plate. The Giflats made a pitching change with Mike Scholz relieving Norlyn Loschen.

In his *News-Gazette* game story, sports writer E.W. Hesse wrote, "With drops of rain already hinting of the imminent downpour, Scholz pitched, Maddock swung and the ball skied high, wide and then deep to center field. G-F outfielder Greg Garland turned and ran back, but the ball was over his head and it bounced over the fence."

Though both runners scored, Osterbur was returned to third base and Maddock was halted at second by a ground-rule double.

Hesse wrote: "But then, even before arguing could develop, rain and wind struck the field, and the fury of it sent the overflow crowd, players, umpires, everyone, scurrying for cover. Before most could reach their cars, the field was inundated and the game — probably the North Division race — was over."

Steve
Maddock

Four years later, on Aug. 14, 1982, in a look back, Hesse wrote, "To this day, Royal fans claim that the ball Maddock hit did not bounce over the fence, but on top of it on its way into the field beyond, and thus should have been ruled a home run. If that was the case, then Royal would have won the game, 3-2, and the North title (with an .821 percentage to the Giflats' .800 percentage)."

Monticello's Rod Schweighart was the winning pitcher in the July 19 All-Star Game at Rantoul as the South edged the North 5-4. Mahomet's Chris Wicks belted a three-run home run for the winners. For the South, Gifford-Flatville had three hits and Royal's Steve Maddock had two hits.

1978 All-Stars:
    Catcher, Scott Rafferty, Gifford-Flatville
    First base, Bob Strohl, Urbana-Champaign
    Second base, Dave Strang, Gifford-Flatville
    Shortstop, Duane Hupp, Monticello
    Third base, Steve Maddock, Royal
    Outfield, Stan Cribbett, Royal
    Outfield, Scott Lockhart, Buckley
    Outfield, Mark Steppe, Mattoon
    Designated hitter, Chris Wicks, Mahomet
    Pitcher, Jerry O'Neill, Royal

Duane
Hupp

Stan
Cribbett

1979

Mike Ellsworth started strong, throwing a no-hitter in the season-opener against Fisher on May 13. He won 8-0.

Gifford-Flatville (23-1) and Mattoon (21-1) dominated the North and South divisions, respectively. Mattoon did so with an offensive juggernaut, averaging 11.5 runs per game. The Giflats had the toughest defense, allowing just 33 runs in 24 games.

Gifford-Flatville's 2-1 playoff win against Mattoon at Royal's Harper Park ended with a classic matchup. With two outs and two runners on base in the ninth inning, batting champion Wade Bradley stepped to the plate to face Pitcher of the Year Mike Scholz.

Bradley's infield groundball was fielded by shortstop Gary Buhr, whose underhand toss to Dave Strang at second base completed a forceout and ended the game.

Neither Scholz (10-0) nor Mattoon's John Widdersheim (9-1) had lost until the game that determined the regular season champion had ended.

Paul Marsillo was the Giflats' hitting star. He singled in Dave Rear with the team's first run and socked a home run to account for the final score. Mattoon's run was scored on Kurt Stretch's sacrifice fly.

The same teams met in the tourney title game. The Giflats posted a 6-5 victory.

1979 managers:

Buckley, Virgil Scheiwe
Decatur, Rudi Escobar and Ray Maulden
Farmer City-Mansfield, Carlos Burton
Fisher, Nick Shepherd and Ron Shepherd
Gifford-Flatville, Dick Franzen and Ralph Loschen
Mahomet, Dan Carlier
Mattoon, Wilbur Diepholz and Monty Stretch
Monticello, Dave Hays
Paxton, Jim Fox
Rantoul, Mike Gallagher and Jack Herbert
Royal, Les Busboom and Mitch Frerichs
Thomasboro, Norm Maier and Gus Robertson
Tolono, Randy McFall
Urbana-Champaign, Bill Warren

Commissioners:

Al Ellsworth, President
Don Cribbett
Ehm Franzen
E.W. Hesse
Lawrence 'Boots' Maier
Don Peters

Stars of the 1970s

Jeff Corley

His E.I. tenure spanned parts of four decades and covered three aspects. Corley was a player in the 1970s and 1980s, a manager in the 1990s and an umpire in the 2000s.

Corley played for — and later coached — Thomasboro. It was no treat, he said, when Gifford-Flatville provided the opposition.

"Facing (Mike) Scholz and (Bob) Harold on a Sunday was tough," Corley said.

He had the opportunity to play with — or against — many of the all-time greats.

Pitcher Kevin Sprau, he said, "was a class act."

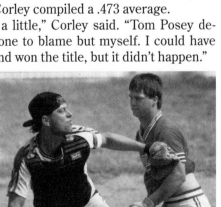

Bob Harold

Corley has a not-so-fond remembrance of the final time they played against each other.

"He struck me out on my last at-bat," Corley said. "It was a 3-2 pitch that was low and outside. Good pitch for Kevin. Bad pitch for me."

Corley said it was no coincidence that Sprau played for successful teams at Buckley, Thomasboro and Rantoul.

"That speaks to what he brought to the teams he played for," Corley said. "Kevin was, and still is, a competitor. I enjoyed playing with him because he always gave it 100 percent."

Corley's best season offensively was in 1976 when he was the runner-up for the batting title. Tom Posey hit .480 and Corley compiled a .473 average.

"Losing the batting title, I was down a little," Corley said. "Tom Posey deserved it. He had a good year. I had no one to blame but myself. I could have walked (on his last at-bat of the season) and won the title, but it didn't happen."

The Thomasboro teams Corley coached won league titles with a nucleus that included pitcher John Harshbarger, catcher Greg Jones, first baseman Bill Elliott, third baseman Bill Wantland and center fielder Jeff Demith.

"Harshbarger was our ace and was fun to play with," Corley said. "He could tell you where a hitter was going to hit a pitch."

Harshbarger's batterymate, Jones, was one of the league's most unflappable characters.

"There was no one like him," Corley

Thomasboro catcher Greg Jones makes a play at the plate.

said. "Greg was Greg. He brought a down-to-earth, play-for-fun attitude but was one of the most competitive people I've ever met. Between the lines, he never wanted to lose. Outside the lines, he had some problems, but he didn't bring them to the ball diamond."

Like Corley, Harshbarger had special praise for Jones.

"He stands out as one of the most physically tough players," Harshbarger said.

During his 15-year career, Jones maintained a .302 career batting average.

As for power, there was no one like Elliott, a left-handed slugger. Corley recalls when the team's newcomer thought about quitting.

Former News-Gazette sportswriter E.W. Hesse

"Some of us old-timers, and his friend Kelly Wetherell (third baseman), talked him out of it," Corley said, "telling him how much fun we had playing for T'boro. He almost quit, but I'm glad he didn't. Those guys were the cornerstone of our '90s championships."

During the first half of Corley's association with the E.I., regular coverage was provided each Monday in *The News-Gazette* sports section by E.W. Hesse, the official league statistician and historian.

"You can't imagine how many people appreciated that," Corley said.

Kevin Sprau

The preeminent pitcher of the 1970s and '80s was the left-hander who grew up in Bellflower in eastern McLean County and later had a tryout with the St. Louis Cardinals. Sprau was the first pitcher to reach 100 documented wins (including postseason play) and the first with more than 1,000 career strikeouts.

His career record was 125-65 and he fashioned 1,164 strikeouts.

Kevin Sprau

"Winning 125 games was a thrill for me," said Sprau, "but you can't have that kind of success unless you have quality teammates around you to make it possible. I was privileged and honored to have played with some of the best."

Sprau's record during his 19-year tenure, which ended in 1990, is unequalled. He fired nine no-hitters, including ones to open the season three successive years: (1974 against Gibson City, 1975 against Tolono and 1976 against Tolono). In each of those seasons, he also came back with a second no-hitter in July.

His 1976 no-hitter was later than others, occurring on June 6. Sprau got a late start that year after he and his wife, Pam, returned from their honeymoon.

In addition to the no-hitters, Sprau had nine one-hitters, 12 two-hitters, 15 three-hitters, 19 four-hitters and 14 five-hitters for a total of 78 low-hit games. He ended his career with 130 complete games, 31 of which were shutouts.

Three times in his career he won both games of a doubleheader, including an Aug. 24, 1977, twin bill against Farmer City-Mansfield in which the second game (a 1-0 victory) was a no-hitter.

Sprau played for Buckley, Rantoul and Thomasboro, having two stints with both Buckley and Rantoul.

He took pride in his overall game. As the designated hitter became a popular choice at all levels to keep weak-hitting pitchers out of the lineup, Sprau was a career .300 hitter (.309 average) who collected more than 200 hits.

"I was not a power hitter but considered myself more of a spray hitter and occasionally liked to lay down the bunt," he said. "I was the leadoff hitter for our fastpitch softball team and gained a lot of experience and knowledge from that, which helped me in the E.I. I was able to see the ball and react to the pitch easier due to the fact it was a greater pitching distance in baseball than softball."

Sprau won his 100th game on Aug. 8, 1984, pitching Buckley to a 9-5 decision against Argenta. He reached the 1,000-strikeout mark in 1985. In 1986, he earned his 100th career regular season victory, June 29 in a 6-3 decision for Buckley against Royal.

One of his most memorable moments, however, didn't center around any pitching achievement.

"One of my biggest thrills was deciding during a game that I was going to bat right-handed because a lefty was pitching, and I got two hits that game," Sprau said. "It was a big thrill because I never practiced batting right-handed and I don't think I ever did it again."

Though he grew up in a community where there are fewer than 500 residents, Sprau wasn't at a disadvantage athletically. His father Lyle, a former E.I. player who died in 2007, transported his son to Farmer City so he could play Little League.

"He was a big part of my success as a baseball player in general," Kevin Sprau said. "His never ending support for me was beyond question. I miss him and think about him every day."

Lyle Sprau was a position player for Bellflower the only year (1938) it fielded a team in the E.I.

"I had no idea when I went to participate in my first E.I. game for Buckley on a warm Wednesday summer day in 1972 that it would be the start of a lot of great memories for me for the next 19 years," Kevin Sprau said.

Kevin Sprau's career pitching chronology:

YEAR	TEAM	W-L	SO	BB	TOURNEY W-L
1972	Buckley	6-0	48	25	1-2
1973	Buckley	7-2	89	38	2-0
1974	Buckley	6-3	87	36	1-1
1975	Rantoul	7-2	91	24	1-1
1976	Rantoul	7-2	107	35	1-1
1977	Thomasboro	6-1	84	32	1-1
1978	Thomasboro	6-6	89	31	1-1

1979	Thomasboro	7-2	66	30	1-0
1980	Thomasboro	9-2	68	26	0-0
1981	Thomasboro	7-6	59	39	0-1
1982	Thomasboro	9-1	45	18	0-0
1983	Thomasboro	7-2	56	25	0-0
1984	Buckley	7-4	63	33	1-1
1985	Buckley	6-2	55	19	2-1
1986	Buckley	5-8	66	28	3-0
1987	Buckley	6-6	62	17	0-0
1988	Buckley	0-0	2	0	0-0
1989	Rantoul	1-2	14	9	0-0
1990	Rantoul	0-4	19	7	1-0
Totals		109-55	1,164	472	16-10

The 1980s

1980

Farmer City-Mansfield's 6 $^1/_2$-year association with the league ended at mid-year when the team could not field enough players to continue. The final 3-25 record included the last 12 losses by forfeit.

Manager Carlos Burton wasn't inactive for long. The first weekend after the team disbanded, he was called to umpire games.

When Opening Day games were played on May 26 two teams posted back-to-back shutouts. Mike Scholz and Dave Gehrke fired consecutive shutouts for Gifford-Flatville in a doubleheader against Paxton. Mattoon Braves' hurlers Gerry Schlecte and Scott Siddens both pitched shutouts against Tolono.

The Mattoon Warriors posted a 22-2 record, concluding a record four consecutive 20-win seasons. Through 2009, no other team has had more than two 20-win seasons in succession.

1981

Mattoon scored twice in the top of the 12th of the tournament championship game to break a tie and edge Champaign 9-7 for the title at Illinois Field. Gerry Schlecte, who pitched the final four innings in relief of John Widdersheim, picked up the victory. Mattoon's first run scored in the top of the 12th when future Major Leaguer Kevin Seitzer — who hadn't pitched all season — walked Darrel Hudson with the bases loaded to force in Mike Holland. Schlecte scored an insurance run on Mike Nichols' sacrifice fly.

Champaign held an 18-10 edge in hits. Rob Phillips, Paul Pierce and Todd Schmitke had three apiece. Nichols and Schlecte each had two hits for the Warriors.

In his *News-Gazette* report, E.W. Hesse wrote, "possibly the smallest finals crowd in E.I. tourney history (100) was present." The low turnout also included the teams. Mattoon had just 10 players in uniform. Champaign was so shorthanded at the start that manager Jack Phillips — whose squad was 44-15 for all games played during the summer — was in right field for the first three innings.

1981 All-Stars:

Catcher, Scott Rafferty, Gifford-Flatville
First base, Bill Elliott, Thomasboro
Second base, Murray Kirby, Thomasboro
Shortstop, Bobby Larson, Thomasboro
Third base, Rick McLain, Rantoul
Left field, Mark McElwain, Gifford-Flatville
Center field, Greg Garland, Gifford-Flatville
Right field, Todd Schmitke, Champaign

Jack Phillips Bobby Larson

Pitchers, (tie) Bruce Scheidegger, Gifford-Flatville; Will Weinhorst, Buckley and John Widdersheim, Mattoon Warriors

1982

Managers:
> Buckley, Virgil Scheiwe
> Champaign, Jack Phillips
> Gifford-Flatville, Dick Franzen and Ralph Loschen
> Danville, Terry Colby, Frank Pitlik and Frank Roose
> Mattoon Braves, Keith Garrett
> Mattoon Warriors, Pat Holland and Wilbur Diepholz
> Monticello, Bob Duncan
> Paxton, Stan Allison
> Rantoul, Phil Herbert
> Royal, Lonnie Freeman and Larry Freeman
> Thomasboro, Marty Kirby
> Tolono, Paul Moore

Commissioners:
> Al Ellsworth, President
> Don Peters, Secretary
> Phil Quinlan, Treasurer
> E.W. Hesse, Statistician
> Ehm Franzen
> Webb Timm

Thomasboro put together what might be considered the most powerful team in league history. The eight position players featured five individuals who at one time were among the league's top seven in season batting average. The group included right fielder Jeff Corley, first baseman Bill Elliott, shortstop Bobby Larson, left fielder Marty Kirby and third baseman Kelly Wetherell.

Midway through the season, T'boro outfielder Tom Broeren was the hitting leader (.489), but an illness sidelined him. In a weakened condition, he returned for the Aug. 15 regular season finale because he was five at-bats short of qualifying for the title. His layoff showed and Broeren was 0 for 7. His averaged dropped to .426, which placed him third, just behind Royal's Mike Johnson (.429). Triple Crown winner Elliott had a league-high .452 batting average.

Collectively, they helped the Indians compile a .353 team batting average for the 26-game regular season schedule, a single-season record.

However, in the tournament championship game, Gifford-Flatville's John Widdersheim shut down the Thomasboro batsmen, pitching his team to a 5-0 victory. He fanned 12 in a four-hit performance. Widdersheim also shut out Buckley in the semifinals, 3-0, on a five-hitter.

John Widdersheim

The 1982 season marked the first time that the designated hitter could be used, for the pitcher only, and that a courtesy runner could be employed for the catcher only.

1983

After playing an interleague All-Star Game for nine of the previous 11 years (with none held in 1977 or 1979), the E.I. entered into a two-year agreement with the Bloomington-based Corn Valley League for a midsummer classic. Both games were held at historic Danville Stadium.

Darrin Fletcher Marty Kirby

Thomasboro's Kevin Sprau was the winning pitcher in the July 22 All-Star Game, an 8-4 E.I. triumph. A year later, Danville's Curt Hughes was the winner as the E.I. prevailed 11-8 on July 6, 1984. Royal's Les Hoveln was 3 for 3 and T'boro's Bobby Larson was 2 for 3. Teenager Darrin Fletcher, from Royal, was 1 for 2.

Both E.I. teams were under the direction of Thomasboro manager Marty Kirby.

Rantoul ended a 16-year association and Champaign dropped out following a two-year stint. Rantoul had a 201-148 regular season record and Champaign was 32-16.

The departures left a nine-team league. In order to get all games scheduled in time for the tournament to start on Aug. 21, a total of 12 week-night doubleheaders were scheduled.

In the Sept. 5 tournament title game at Gifford, Thomasboro's John Harshbarger pitched Thomasboro to a 2-0 win against the Giflats. The teams had shared the regular season crown with 25-7 records though G-F won the regular season series with T'boro, 3-1.

Greg Jones broke up the scoreless duel in the seventh inning, racing home on a single by Jeff Demith.

The 25 wins by the Giflats and the Indians remain the single-season standard for regular season victories entering the summer of 2010.

1983 All-Stars:

    Catcher, Eric Thiel, Thomasboro
    First base, Bill Elliott, Thomasboro
    Second base, Steve Darnell, Danville
    Shortstop, Gary Buhr, Gifford-Flatville
    Third base, Les Hoveln, Royal
    Left field, Phil Scheiwe, Buckley
    Center field, Mike Holland, Mattoon
    Right field, Craig Nichols, Tolono
    Designated hitter, Chris Slack, Monticello
    Pitcher, John Widdersheim, Gifford-Flatville

Craig Nichols Gary Buhr

1984

Gifford-Flatville (20-11) built an 8-0 lead on Buckley in the Sept. 3 title game before holding on for an 11-10 triumph. The game was played on Labor Day after rain wiped out Buckley's 2-0 lead a day earlier and forced the game to be replayed in its entirety.

Howie Walker Les Hoveln

Catching Up

Mark McElwain, Dave Rear and Howie Walker all homered for the Gilfats.
The Giflats' starting lineup:

Catcher, Paul Pierce
First base, Howie Walker
Second base, Dave Strang
Shortstop, Gary Buhr
Third base, Dave Rear
Left field, Dave Lamb
Center field, Mike Holland
Right field, Tim Gasparich
Designated hitter, Mark McElwain
Pitcher, John Widdersheim

Paul Pierce

Others who played were Mike Seibold, as the courtesy runner, Greg Rogers, who provided four innings of relief, and Wilson Ortiz, who filled in at first base. In the semifinals, left-hander Rogers pitched all nine innings as G-F topped Danville 10-5.

In a regular season twin bill sweep at Royal, Pierce enjoyed a 5 for 6 day, belting three home runs and knocking in 10 runs.

The largest reported crowd of the season was at Danville Stadium for a

Gifford-Flatville All-Star Dave Rear avoids a tag by Thomasboro third baseman Kelly Wetherell.

May 26 doubleheader between Danville and Tolono. The announced attendance was 3,339. Danville teammates Steve Darnell and Greg Thompson each had three hits in each game.

One of the league's best-pitched games was played at Gifford on June 17. Argenta's Kent Clements no-hit the Giflats, outdueling Rogers in a 1-0 thriller. Rogers allowed five hits, all singles. Argenta's lone run was in the fifth inning when Roger Hupp drove in his brother, Larry Hupp.

Kent Clements

Following his gem, his first since Pony League, Clements was quoted in *The News-Gazette* saying, "I was intimidated after the first game (when the Giflats had 12 hits). They were really hitting ropes. I mainly tried to keep the ball down so they'd hit it on the ground."

On July 8, Gifford-Flatville's Dale Schweighart ended the 24-game hitting streak of Tolono's Craig Nichols, whose streak began in July of 1983.

On Aug. 8, less than a month after his 31st birthday, Buckley's Kevin Sprau became the first member of the 100-win club. In a Wednesday night game at Urbana's Prairie Park, he pitched the Dutch Masters past Argenta 9-5, raising his career record to 100-40. Teammates Troy Genzel and Phil Herbert each had three hits in the game.

The league's cumulative batting average (covering all players) was a record .296, breaking the record established the year before (.288). The final composite batting averages for specified years:

1951	.244	1964	.258
1974	.259	1984	.296

1985

John Harshbarger, the dominant pitcher during the regular season, was virtually untouchable in the postseason. In 23 tournament innings, he allowed one earned run while winning three times to complete his 13-0 season.

Thomasboro pitcher John Harshbarger

He stymied Buckley on a two-hitter in the finals, with T'boro posting a 10-1 triumph. Greg Jones homered for Thomasboro. Jones had two hits as did teammates Murray Kirby and Bill Elliott. In the semis, Elliott was 3 for 3 and Jeff Demith was 2 for 3 in a 6-0 win against Rantoul.

T'boro's summer roster: Jeff Bowers, Tom Broeren, Troy Burgess, Kent Clements, Troy Cunningham, Jeff Demith, Joe Dunham, Bill Elliott, Rick Filippo, Chuck Foran, John Harshbarger, Duff Hoel, Greg Jones, Murray Kirby, Bobby Larson, Kurt Simmons, Mike Stremming, Rick Swearingen and Shawn Wildermuth.

Thomasboro runner Chuck Foran slides into base.

When the season openers were played on May 12, Danville's Steve Darnell showed he was ready to go from the outset. He was 8 for 9 in a twin bill at Royal raising his Opening Day stats for a three-year period to 19 for 26 (.731 average). One of the summer's top games was played May 26 in Rantoul. Pitchers Duane Johnson (Royal) and Ken Koebrich (Rantoul) allowed three total hits. Royal's 1-0 win was courtesy of Darrin Fletcher's two-out double in the top of the seventh. His hit — the only one the Giants managed against Koebrich — drove in Brian Remington. For Koebrich, a left-hander, it was the first of three consecutive games he lost when Rantoul was held scoreless.

At season's end, Koebrich's record was 5-8, but five of the losses were games in which his team was held scoreless.

Another noteworthy game took place on June 22 at Rantoul. Brothers Stan Paul and Tom Paul were matched up in a game that required 10 innings before Stan's Tolono team posted a 7-4 victory.

Each brother pitched nine innings with Stan walking three and fanning eight

Rick Swearingen

Duane Johnson

Stan Paul

Tom Paul

Richard Paul

Rick Filippo

Barry Elson

Catching Up

while yielding four hits. Stan pitched out of a bases-loaded, no outs jam in the bottom of the ninth. Tom was touched for seven hits. He walked one and struck out four. Another brother, first baseman Richard Paul, hit a two-run home run in the ninth inning for Tolono, which sent the game into extra innings.

In a four-week midseason span, *The News-Gazette* used a radar gun to time the velocity of 29 pitchers. Thomasboro had the three fastest hurlers: Kent Clements and Rick Filippo each hit 87 mph and John Harshbarger hit 86. Rounding out the five fastest were Tolono's Barry Elson (85 mph) and Gifford-Flatville's Mike Scholz (85 mph).

1985 All-Stars:
> Catcher, John Patrizi, Tolono
> First base, Kenton Carley, Buckley
> Second base, Murray Kirby, Thomasboro
> Shortstop, Rod Wallace, Royal
> Third base, Chris Slack, Tolono
> Outfield, Herman Cunningham, Danville
> Outfield, Jeff Demith, Thomasboro
> Outfield, K.K. Turner, Danville
> Designated hitter, Jeff Krumwiede, Tolono
> Utility, Kevin Johnson, Paxton
> Right-handed pitcher, John Harshbarger, Thomasboro
> Left-handed pitcher, Kevin Sprau, Buckley

1986

The season's highest scoring game took place on May 25 when Tolono hammered eight home runs in a 20-12 triumph at Rantoul. Chris Slack led the way, going 4 for 4 with each of his hits landing for home runs. The home runs came on consecutive at-bats. John Patrizi hit two out of the park while teammates Scott Goins and Jeff Krumwiede each had one. Goins was also 4 for 4.

David Scott

Gifford-Flatville pitcher Greg Rogers.

One of the more interesting games was the second game of a doubleheader on June 8 at Rantoul where Thomasboro defeated Danville 4-1. Each of the T'boro runs came on solo home runs. Bill Elliott and Greg Jones each hit two home runs. The team's only other hit against David Scott was a single by Joe Dunham. Rick Filippo pitched six innings and scattered five hits.

Greg Rogers, a 23-year-old left-hander, threw his first career no-hitter — including Little League — leading Gifford-Flatville to a 5-0 win against Tolono on June 29. Mark McElwain's three-run homer in the first inning provided Rogers all the offensive support he would need.

Kevin Sprau added to his legacy, pitching Buckley to an 8-3 championship-game victory against Danville in the tournament finals. It was the first time he was the winning pitcher in a tournament title game. He pitched all three of the Dutch Masters' postseason wins, evening his season record at 8-8. Against a Danville team which played 60 games for the summer (ending 41-19), Sprau allowed seven hits and struck out five. Teammate Tim Kemmer went 5 for 5 to lead the Dutch Masters' offensive assault. Mark Scheiwe knocked in five runs.

Kevin Dallas

Buckley's tournament roster: Kenton Carley, Andy Cotner, Troy Genzel, Tim Kemmer, Paul Lindauer, Scott Lockhart, Eddie Moore, Steve Nuss, Doug Post, Ron Rieches, Mark Scheiwe, Kevin Sprau and Dwain Warrens. Brothers Mark and Phil Scheiwe joined their father, Virgil, as the team's coaches.

1987

The year's biggest comeback happened on July 19 when Paxton rallied from an 11-3 deficit with an 11-run outburst in the bottom of the sixth. Kevin Dallas, who was 6 for 6 in the twin bill, had four hits and three RBI to lead the comeback. Teammate Phil Hull had three hits,

Roger Kingston

including the single that put Paxton ahead to stay.

Ironically, Paxton was on the opposite end of the biggest one-inning outburst of the season. In an Aug. 23 game, Royal expanded a 4-1 lead with a 13-run inning in the top of the seventh. Dave Allen and Perry Dable each had three hits for the Giants.

Tolono pitcher Gail Ring

Six games into the season, Paxton lost one of its key players when outfielder Roger Kingston was signed to a free agent contract by the Cleveland Indians and assigned to Batavia, N.Y. For the Swedes, Kingston was off to a .315 start.

Joe Dunham

Ed Logan

The most unusual situation occurred when Gail Ring pitched two complete seven-inning games in Tolono's Aug. 8 doubleheader sweep at Danville. However, due to rain, the second game was not played until Aug. 23. Ring struck out five batters in Game 1 and 10 in the second game.

Thomasboro second baseman Murray Kirby

In the championship game on Sept. 7, Thomasboro scored seven runs in the last three innings to overcome Rantoul's 3-1 lead and post an 8-4 triumph. Brian Innis pitched a complete game and earned the win. Bill Elliott, Duff Hoel and Paul Pierce all had two hits for T'boro.

The tournament was a time for revenge for the Indians. During the regular season, three opponents swept doubleheaders from T'boro: Danville, Royal and Rantoul. Those were the three teams Thomasboro defeated in the postseason by a combined 22-5 margin.

Two squad members retired following the title-game victory: second baseman Murray Kirby and right fielder Chuck Foran.

1987 All-Stars:
Catcher, Brad Allen, Royal
First base, Jeff Thompson, Danville
Second base, Dave Strang, Gifford-Flatville
Shortstop, Kevin Kasper, Rantoul
Third base, Les Hoveln, Royal
Outfield, Jeff Demith, Thomasboro
Outfield, Joe Dunham, Thomasboro
Outfield, Dave Gibson, Buckley
Designated hitter, Mark McElwain, Gifford-Flatville
Utility, Mike Walling, Paxton
Right-handed pitcher, Ed Logan, Rantoul
Left-handed pitcher, Ken Koebrich, Rantoul

1988

Buckley's Dutch Masters got stronger the longer the postseason tournament lasted. Buckley needed extra innings to outlast a 10-18 Thomasboro team 7-6 in the quarterfinals. Eddie Moore pitched all 10 innings. In the semifinals, the Dutch Masters handled 15-14 Rantoul 13-3. Moore pitched eight innings and, for the second consecutive game, walked no one. Eric LaVoie had a 1-2-3 ninth inning.

Eric LaVoie

Bill Wantland

Greg Jones

In the title game, Moore improved his overall record to 14-3 as Buckley overpowered an 18-12 Tolono team 17-4. Moore worked eight innings and LaVoie entered in the ninth and threw 10 of his 12 pitches in the strike zone, fanning two and yielding one hit.

Dave Strang

Terry Colby

William 'Smokey' Karr

Cleanup hitter LaVoie cleaned up at the plate. He was 4 for 5 in the quarter-finals, 3 for 4 in the semifinals and 4 for 5 in the championship contest. Five of his 11 tournament hits were for extra bases and he drove in nine runs. He also walked twice and reached base on 13 of 16 plate appearances.

Teammate Dave Gibson (8 for 14) was another hot postseason hitter. In the title game, leadoff hitter Tim Kemmer was 3 for-5 and walked once.

When the season began, three athletes had played in at least 100 consecutive regular season games: Gifford-Flatville's Bill Wantland (146), Thomasboro's Greg Jones (109) and the Giflats' Dave Strang (102). At season's end, Strang retired following a standout 13-year career. He ranks fifth in career hits (376).

For the first time, the league experimented with three-man umpiring

Umpires John Johnston, left, and Gary Gebauer

crews during the season. Managers approved the change by a 7-1 vote in the pre-season with Paxton the lone dissenter. The following year, however, the league returned to two-man officiating crews. Two of the league's veteran umpires were Gary Gebauer and John Johnston.

1988 managers:
    Buckley, Scott Lockhart
    Danville, Terry Colby
    Gifford-Flatville, Gary Buhr, Dick Franzen and Ralph Loschen
    Paxton, Tom Scott
    Rantoul, Doug Quinlan
    Royal, Les Hoveln and Steve Maddock
    Thomasboro, Jeff Demith and Bill Elliott
    Tolono, Keith Garrett and Paul Moore
Commissioners:
    Al Ellsworth, President
    Wes Hethke, Secretary
    Phil Quinlan, Treasurer
    Fred Kroner, Statistician
    William 'Smokey' Karr

1989

Bob Harold pitched six innings of relief and picked up his second postseason win as Gifford-Flatville (which started the season 2-7) over-

Gifford-Flatville pitcher Bob Harold

powered Tolono 7-1 in the Sept. 3 title game at Tolono. Gary Buhr, Greg Fitzgerald, Kyle Herges, C.R. Black and Rick Wyninger all had two hits for G-F. Ken Whited had three hits for Tolono and future major league umpire Mark Carlson had two hits for the Aces.

Harold, 35, was in his second year back in the E.I. following an eight-year layoff. The Giflats finished with a 17-10 E.I. record and a 33-12 overall mark.

The Giflats' starting lineup for the title game:
    Catcher, C.R. Black
    First base, Kyle Herges
    Second base, Gary Buhr
    Shortstop, Dave Allen
    Third base, Matt Herges
    Left field, Greg Fitzgerald
    Center field, Rick Wyninger
    Right field, Chris Hammack
    Designated hitter, Tony Ewing
    Pitcher, Bob Harold

Gifford-Flatville's Dave Allen, left

The Giflats' Buhr, playing in his 19th E.I. season, registered his 400th career hit in June. It came against the same pitcher who also yielded No. 300: Thomasboro's Barry Elson. In his career, Buhr played on 16 teams that won either the regular season or tournament championships (or both).

Thomasboro put 30 runs on the scoreboard in a regular season doubleheader sweep at Paxton without the benefit of a home run among its 37 hits. Leadoff hitter Joe Dunham was 7 for 7 for the day, walked three times and stole four bases. Jeff Demith and Bill Elliott each had five hits for the day. T'boro won 16-7 and 14-2.

Gary Buhr

Darrin Kregel

The year's best-played contest was on July 16, when Paxton's Brad Forsyth scored in the bottom of the seventh on Jeff Rutledge's single to edge rival Buckley 1-0. Neither team committed an error and there were no extra-base hits. Darrin Kregel fired a one-hitter and outdueled Eddie Moore in the opening game of a doubleheader, which marked the 200th regular season victory for the Swedes. The second game was not so tame. Buckley erupted for 16 hits and won 13-9.

Buckley's Moore and Todd Post (with one inning of relief help from Troy Elias) pitched back-to-back shutouts on July 30 at home against Gifford-Flatville. Moore walked no one in a five-hit, 4-0 victory in the opener. Post and Elias teamed up to hold the Giflats hitless in the nightcap. Tim Kemmer, Phil Scheiwe and Dave Gibson each had two hits for Buckley for the afternoon.

In the Aug. 12 All-Star Game with the Danville Twilight League, Joe Dunham (Thomasboro) and Mark Scheiwe (Buckley) each had three hits as the E.I. posted a resounding 18-1 conquest. Jeff Demith (Thomasboro) hit the game's only home run. Bob Harold (Giflats), Brian Innis (Thomasboro) and Greg Rogers (Giflats) each pitched three innings, teaming up for a six-hitter and nine strikeouts. Starter Harold was the winner. Kenny Young had three hits for the Twilight team.

1989 All-Stars:

Catcher, C.R. Black, Gifford-Flatville
First base, Bill Elliott, Thomasboro
Second base, Bill Wantland, Thomasboro
Shortstop, Duff Hoel, Thomasboro
Third base, Ken Whited, Tolono
Outfield, Jeff Demith, Thomasboro
Outfield, Dave Murray, Tolono
Outfield, Jerome Nelson, Tolono
Designated hitter, Troy Cunningham, Tolono
Right-handed pitcher, Eddie Moore, Buckley
Left-handed pitcher, Ken Koebrich, Tolono

Duff Hoel

Eddie Moore

Ken Koebrich

Stars of the 1980s

Darrin Fletcher

Before he played 1,245 games in the major leagues, Darrin Fletcher played dozens of games for Royal in the Eastern Illinois Baseball League. With a grandfather (Glen Fletcher) and a father (Tom Fletcher) who were prominent E.I. players, there were plenty of reasons to believe the left-handed hitting catcher who graduated from Oakwood High School would carry on the family legacy.

As a teenager, halfway through his prep career, young Fletcher was suiting up for the Royal Giants.

Royal catcher Darrin Fletcher, left, makes the tag on Gifford-Flatville's Tim Gasparich.

"I did it on purpose," father Tom said. "Physically he was big enough and I wanted to see what he could do."

Questions were answered in Fletcher's first E.I. at-bat.

"His first swing was a ground-rule double," Tom Fletcher said. "He fit right in."

Darrin Fletcher went on to star for the University of Illinois before becoming a sixth-round draft choice in 1987 by the Los Angeles Dodgers.

"People thought I was over my head when I entered (the E.I.) at 15," Darrin Fletcher said. "There were college pitchers and older veterans; guys who knew how to play and were very competitive. When I had success, that gave me confidence. I think it prepared me to make the next step to the U of I."

His mind-set was the main reason.

"If I could hit college pitching at 15, I didn't see any reason I couldn't hit it at 18," he said.

Fletcher had grown up with the E.I. League.

"I was a batboy for Royal when my dad played and they won the league," he said. "I used to go to Royal and watch a lot of games. I thought I was ready. Maybe I was an over-confident teenager. Looking back, there were a lot of good players and maybe I shouldn't have been so confident."

He appreciated the opportunities, and not just when he was swinging a bat. One of the Giants' pitchers was left-hander Jerry O'Neill, who had an extensive minor league background that included a year in Class AAA (1974) and 107 minor league appearances in parts of six seasons.

"Working with a guy who'd played professionally was a great experience," said Darrin Fletcher, whose career E.I. average was .339 between 1982-87.

He found opposing pitchers treated him like any other squad member.

"They didn't take it easy on me," he said. "It was a man's league and they treated me like a man."

Part of the time he played for Royal, he was also a member of Danville's American Legion baseball team. His loyalty was with the adult team.

"My dad told the Legion people that E.I. took precedence," Darrin Fletcher said. "It was a family tradition. Some of my fondest memories of amateur ball were those Sunday doubleheaders."

Tom Fletcher said his son also benefitted from having former catchers involved with the Royal team as coaches.

"Larry Freeman taught Darrin a lot about catching," Tom Fletcher said.

Darrin Fletcher, a 6-foot-1 left-handed hitter, played 14 years in the major leagues, spending time with Los Angeles, Philadelphia, Montreal and Toronto. He retired on July 16, 2002, two years after a season in which he batted .320 and swatted 20 home runs with the Blue Jays.

Jeff Demith

For more than a decade, Jeff Demith had the perfect position in the Thomasboro batting order. He was the No. 3 hitter and was followed to the plate by Bill Elliott, who set the career home run record before retiring. Pitchers wouldn't work around Demith and he responded by compiling a .366 career batting average and breaking the all-time record for hits (461).

"Breaking the record was never a goal or ambition I ever thought about," Demith said.

Jeff Demith

The opportunity to participate in America's national pastime was all the motivation Demith needed.

"E.I. baseball was a chance to keep playing a sport that I loved with my whole heart and a chance to play with guys whom I respected and called my friends," Demith said. "Statistics were fun to look at and something you could compare yourself to other guys in the league, but that was never a driving force. We just looked forward to every weekend with great anticipation and prayed that the weather would cooperate. Playing and competing was the driving force."

Even after many of his veteran teammates such as Elliott and Bill Wantland retired, Demith found the motivation to continue playing in the league.

"I loved the game. I loved the league. I wanted to play forever," Demith said. "Not for the records, but for the joy of the game and the camaraderie of the team."

During the period Wantland was chasing the hits record, held previously by Gary Buhr, Thomasboro faithful constructed a board known as the Wantland

Watch. It had a current countdown for how many hits were needed for the record.

"When he finally broke the record, it was big news and the celebration went into the night," Demith recalled. "At that time, I still never thought about breaking the record."

Media interest in the E.I. had waned somewhat by the time Demith was approaching his hits milestone.

"There was no chase, no big publicity," he said. "Just me and the love I had for the game."

The record books reveal the hits mark is still held by Demith. He doesn't view himself in that regard.

"I don't see myself as the all-time hits leader," Demith said. "I see myself as a guy who had a solid career, who had his share of hits and who played a long time. There have been lots of better hitters than me who went through the league, but none who played as long as me."

Demith believes one of his younger T'boro teammates — Ken Crawford — would have surpassed his hits record had he matched Demith's longevity.

"Ken would hold the record if he had played longer," Demith said.

Former Thomasboro manager Marty Kirby recruited Demith to play for the Indians after watching him perform with Parkland College. Kirby's father, Merwin, was also instrumental in the young athlete being able to stay in town during the summer instead of returning to his native Chicago Heights.

"He gave me a job so I could stay down here and play those first few summers," Demith said.

A special thanks, Demith said, must go out to Elliott.

"He hit behind me all of those years and made sure I got my share of fastballs," Demith said, "because if you knew E.I., you knew Bill Elliott."

Pitchers would much rather take their chances facing Demith than trying to battle Elliott with runners on base. It was considered the lesser of two evils.

"E.I. baseball wasn't just baseball," Demith said. "It was a way of life for nearly 18 years, and I wouldn't trade any of them."

Jeff Demith's career batting chronology:

YEAR	TEAM	AB	R	H	2B	3B	HR	AVG.
1983	Thomasboro	91	25	30	7	1	1	.330
1984	Thomasboro	80	21	32	6	0	5	.400
1985	Thomasboro	84	31	32	7	2	2	.381
1986	Thomasboro	93	34	36	6	1	6	.387
1987	Thomasboro	85	28	33	11	1	7	.388
1988	Thomasboro	88	32	40	2	1	8	.455
1989	Thomasboro	77	26	28	7	1	5	.364
1990	Thomasboro	69	11	15	2	0	5	.217
1991	Thomasboro	63	19	24	4	1	3	.381
1992	Thomasboro	62	23	29	6	0	3	.467
1993	Thomasboro	76	28	31	7	1	2	.408
1994	Thomasboro	69	16	24	8	0	3	.348

Catching Up

1995	Thomasboro	75	20	24	4	1	7	.320
1996	Thomasboro	79	28	28	1	0	4	.354
1997	Thomasboro	60	18	20	4	2	3	.333
1998	Thomasboro	67	14	19	0	0	2	.284
1999	Thomasboro	19	6	5	0	0	1	.263
2000	Thomasboro	21	7	11	2	0	0	.524
Totals		1258	387	461	84	12	67	.366

Bill Elliott

Those who watched the mammoth home runs that Bill Elliott swatted during his years with Thomasboro wouldn't be surprised to learn that he played part of the 1979 season for the Cincinnati Reds' minor league team in Eugene, Ore.

And yet, there is a surprise.

Elliott tried to make it professionally as a pitcher.

"In the minors, I had one at-bat and hit into a double play," Elliott said.

The Decatur native returned to central Illinois and enrolled at Parkland College at the urging of former Cobra baseball coach Jim Reed. His roommates were Bill Wantland, who played for Buckley, and Kelly Wetherell, who was looking for a summer-league baseball team.

Bill Elliott

Parkland's assistant coach, John Harshbarger, had pitched for T'boro and directed both Elliott and Wetherell to the Indians along with two other Parkland athletes, Paul Pierce and Shawn Stahl.

T'boro first gave Elliott a shot on the mound, with Stahl playing at first base.

"I was wild as ever those first couple of starts with T'boro," said Elliott, who averaged more than a walk per inning while pitching in the minors. "I was just a big, hard-throwing wild left-hander. I was never a true pitcher, as I got to see in my years playing E.I. baseball."

An injury to Stahl enabled Elliott to shift permanently to his more natural position, first base. The following year, Stahl and Pierce elected to play for a Champaign team in the E.I., coached by Jack Phillips, and Elliott became a fixture in the cleanup position and at first base with Thomasboro.

The rest, as the saying goes, is history.

Before retiring, Elliott set still-standing single-season (13 in 1983) and career (100) home run records in the E.I.

"The thing I remember most was all the great fans that came out," Elliott said. "They made the rivalries so much more intense and exciting. There was nothing better than the sidelines full of fans and everybody clinging to every play, cheering for their team, but more so trying to get you off your game by hollering at you. It worked on most of the players, but for the few who excelled in E.I. baseball, it did the opposite and made you excel even more."

Two pitchers in particular were Elliott's main nemeses.

"Kevin Sprau seemed to throw a hundred different pitches from all different angles," Elliott said. "Now that was a pitcher. His arm seemed to get stronger as the game went on."

In the same category was former Gifford-Flatville ace Bob Harold.

"I don't think there was a better pitcher in his prime than Bob," Elliott said. "That slider that he threw was as tough of a pitch to hit as anything."

Elliott recalled facing another Gifford-Flatville ace, Mike Scholz.

"I could see why he was the top player in E.I. history," Elliott said. "What a tremendous competitor. I hit a home run against him early in my career, with Scott Rafferty catching. I got a little cocky and stood there and watched it go out, then had a little flip of the bat before I took off. Both of them were cussing me around the bases and telling me I was going down the next time up. Sure enough, I got hit on the right knee on the first pitch. The Gifford fans were cheering as I gimped down to first base."

While teammate Jeff Demith was best known for shattering the career hits record, Elliott recognized an overlooked aspect of the center fielder's game.

"There was no one better at going after a fly ball," Elliott said. "There were so many times that a ball was going to the gap and he ran it down when everybody thought it was at least a double."

Bill Elliott's career batting chronology:

YEAR	TEAM	AB	R	H	2B	3B	HR	AVG.
1980	Thomasboro	65	21	24	7	0	7	.369
1981	Thomasboro	69	17	29	6	0	5	.420
1982	Thomasboro	84	27	38	10	2	9	.452
1983	Thomasboro	98	31	36	8	0	13	.367
1984	Thomasboro	81	9	23	7	1	0	.284
1985	Thomasboro	99	24	29	6	0	8	.293
1986	Thomasboro	74	19	32	2	0	7	.432
1987	Thomasboro	74	10	22	4	0	2	.297
1988	Thomasboro	59	12	23	2	0	3	.390
1989	Thomasboro	79	20	30	9	0	7	.380
1990	Thomasboro	71	13	20	3	0	4	.282
1991	Thomasboro	38	9	12	2	0	3	.316
1992	Thomasboro	67	13	23	4	0	6	.343
1993	Thomasboro	74	19	28	4	0	7	.378
1994	Did Not Play							
1995	Thomasboro	82	19	33	5	0	8	.402
1996	Thomasboro	86	17	26	2	0	9	.302
1997	Thomasboro	8	3	4	0	0	2	.500

Totals		1208	283	432	81	3	100	.358

Bill Wantland

He was a combination of the best aspects of Ty Cobb and Pete Rose. Bill Wantland was the epitome of tenacity and hustle on the baseball diamond.

He was known for head-first slides, wearing a batting helmet on the base paths and sprinting to first base following a walk.

The Sunday success stories were there for all who watched E.I. League baseball to see.

Most don't realize what took place behind the scenes.

"I spent many a Monday so sore I could barely move," Wantland said, "let alone go up those stairs in my house. I used a couple hundred vacation days at work, for Mondays off."

Wantland has no regrets.

"I would do it all over again," he said.

Baseball brought out the passion in Wantland, a Danville native.

Bill Wantland

"I would wake up on Sunday mornings early, knowing I was going to play a doubleheader," he said. "I was wired from 8 a.m. until the first pitch. Then I would turn into this focused monster on the field, who knew only one way to play: Hard."

His was a no-holds-barred attitude.

"Even though I personally knew half the players on the other teams we played each Sunday, I had no friends until the game was over," Wantland said. "That was just how I played."

It's not surprising that comparisons to Wantland start with Rose, especially since Wantand chose to wear uniform No. 14, like his childhood idol.

"Talk about a guy who earned his money playing every game with spirit and hustle," Wantland said. "Just a normal base hit to center field and he is running as hard as he can to first, then rounds the base hard, looking for an opportunity to take second because of a bobble or an outfielder not hustling the ball back in."

Wantland loved to emulate that style.

"I wasn't fast, but I knew I could help my team by playing like Pete," he said. "I loved to dive. My head-first slides were almost dives. Playing defense, taking away base hits with a dive, then throwing them out was awesome."

Wantland played primarily at second base or third base throughout his career.

"I remember several times thinking, 'I can't get that one, but I will see how close I can come,'" he said. "Sure enough, I would watch it into my glove and think, 'Holy Cow! I made that play.' I always looked at the player who hit it and said, 'You should not have hit it this way.'"

Former Thomasboro first baseman Bill Elliott remembered the way Wantland would challenge hitters.

"He would play up on the grass at third and dare you to hit it by him," Elliott said. "He was so intense. You loved him on your team and hated him on the other team."

Buckley's Trent Eshleman confirms that feeling.

"Billy added to his means of drawing attention to himself by donning a hard batting helmet while playing the field," Eshleman said. "He drew further attention by being an emotional player that would mix in a fist pump after getting a hit or making a good play in the field. All of this made me despise the man in my youth as a player, but I grew to respect what he stood for as I became a veteran player in the league."

Wantland's introduction to the E.I. came in 1978, when he was playing for the University of Illinois under coach Tom Dedin. Following a scrimmage at Illinois Field (then located near the intersection of Wright and University streets in Urbana), former Buckley manager Virgil Scheiwe asked Wantland about playing for the Dutch Masters.

"I am so grateful to have played for Virgil," Wantland said, "as I still believe he should have been a major league manager.

"He had that charisma that just beamed baseball."

Wantland played nine years for the Dutch Masters, leaving for Gifford-Flatville and the chance to play more at second base. He left one organization with an all-star manager for another with a leader who was equally respected.

Ralph Loschen

"Ralph Loschen was to Gifford what Virgil Scheiwe was to Buckley," Wantland said. "Professional people who loved baseball and wanted to see baseball played proudly in their town."

Eshleman echoed Wantland's sentiments.

"The grandfather of the E.I. League," Eshleman said. "Ralph is one of my most respected people in the game of baseball for his extreme love and commitment to baseball."

Wantland stayed with the Giflats three summers but was unable to help the team win a regular season pennant or a tournament championship.

"That became my driving force to continue playing E.I. baseball," Wantland said.

Making the decision to change teams for a second time was a tough call to make.

"Telling Ralph that I was leaving Gifford to play for Thomasboro was one of the hardest phone calls I ever had to make," Wantland said. "I could hear and feel the disappointment in his voice."

While with Thomasboro for 10 seasons, Wantland broke the career hits record, played for one regular season titlist and three tournament champions, but another memory is etched prominently in his mind.

"Two different people, Billy Babb and Paul Kilgore, came to games and brought a son and a grandson," Wantland said. "They both proceeded to tell me they wanted those boys to watch me play the game and that was how they should play the game. Those were the kinds of things that made the E.I. League special to me."

As his career .324 batting average would indicate, Wantland wasn't stymied by too many pitchers. One in particular, however, was a constant thorn in his side.

"Chip (Greg) Immke (from Royal) gave me fits," Wantland said. "He was a lefty, too, and I loved hitting off lefties, but I don't think I ever got a hit off of him."

While with the Indians, Wantland was able to play alongside two of the league's all-time greats.

"Ken Crawford may have been the best hitter I ever played with or against," Wantland said. "In my opinion, he was out of our league and deserved a shot at higher baseball. Everything he hit was peas.

"Jeff Demith was a blast to play for, with and against. Jeff is so fast and could leg out those infielder dribblers where I would get thrown out."

For many of the summers Wantland devoted to E.I. League baseball, he had a special fan in the stands.

"My wife, Clydette, eventually made regular appearances at almost every game, bringing the kids and cheering me on, as best friends do," he said. "Then, she had to listen to me complain for two days about how sore I was."

Bill Wantland's career batting chronology:

YEAR	TEAM	AB	R	H	2B	3B	HR	AVG.
1978	Buckley	28	7	9	2	0	0	.321
1979	Buckley	66	10	23	2	1	1	.348
1980	Buckley	69	14	26	7	1	1	.377
1981	Buckley	71	15	19	2	0	2	.268
1982	Buckley	83	16	25	3	1	0	.301
1983	Buckley	104	19	34	7	1	0	.327
1984	Buckley	90	21	28	2	1	2	.311
1985	Buckley	83	16	28	7	1	2	.337
1986	Gifford-Flatville	76	14	30	2	0	0	.395
1987	Gifford-Flatville	89	23	28	3	1	2	.315
1988	Gifford-Flatville	86	16	25	5	0	1	.291
1989	Thomasboro	79	21	26	6	0	1	.329
1990	Thomasboro	77	14	22	2	0	2	.286
1991	Thomasboro	61	12	13	6	0	0	.213
1992	Thomasboro	58	9	18	1	0	0	.310

Year	Team							
1993	Thomasboro	75	19	24	7	0	1	.320
1994	Thomasboro	65	15	21	3	0	2	.323
1995	Thomasboro	66	13	24	4	0	2	.364
1996	Thomasboro	67	15	26	7	0	1	.388
1997	Thomasboro	9	2	5	0	0	0	.556
1998	Did Not Play							
1999	Thomasboro	8	2	3	0	0	1	.375
Totals		1410	293	457	78	7	21	.324

K.K. Turner

His actions spoke volumes about the respect he held for the Eastern Illinois Baseball League.

While playing collegiately at Eastern Illinois University, Turner had the option of participating in a New York-based summer league. He thanked EIU head coach Tom McDevitt for the chance, but graciously declined.

"Talent is talent," Turner said.

He saw no reason to spend

K.K. Turner

his summer hundreds of miles from his family when he could remain locally and face what he regarded as an equally challenging schedule with quality competition.

"There were definitely a number of pitchers in the (E.I.) league that could knock the bat out of your hands," Turner said. "Even though there were a lot of college pitchers in the league, there were guys pitching that were in their mid-20s and early 30s.

"I wasn't used to seeing the precision pitches like hard sliders and sharp curveballs on the black. Those were pitches that many young college pitchers were not able to master.

"Overall, year in and year out, the caliber of play in the E.I. was the best that I have ever played with. The college teams may have had more depth at pitching, however the collective grade of the E.I. was a few percent better than many D-I teams."

Turner played his first game for the Danville Roosters as an 18-year-old. His debut was a memorable one.

"My very first at-bat at Danville Stadium was a home run," Turner said.

It was a sign of what was to come. Despite carrying only about 155 pounds on his 5-foot-8 frame, Turner wound up as the Roosters' all-time home run leader (27).

"As a kid, I never thought that I would play on the same field that Cecil Cooper,

Gorman Thomas, Darrell Porter, Dick Davis, Bill Castro, Pedro Guerrero and many other major leaguers had played on," Turner said. "Danville Stadium was a beautiful place to play when the groundskeeper kept it up, which was most of the time."

Years after the community had lost its minor league affiliate, the Roosters helped fill the baseball void.

"The stadium and the team gave the folks in Danville and the surrounding areas an opportunity to continue the rich tradition of Saturday night baseball in central Illinois," Turner said. "I distinctly remember promotional nights where there would be 1,500 to 3,000 people in attendance. I could not believe there were actually people paying to watch the team play. The fans were very cordial to the players. I remember signing autographs for individuals of all ages."

Danville preferred to play its E.I. games on Saturday nights — when the crowds would be larger — than on Sunday afternoons. During the first six years of this policy (1982-87), the home team had a clear advantage. Danville won 62 percent of its night games but only 48 percent of its afternoon games.

Turner played from 1982 to 1988, spending his final two seasons with Rantoul. He had something to prove as he switched teams.

K.K. Turner

"Danville told me that I was done," Turner recalled. "Rod Peavler (Rantoul manager) gave me my second wind. Rod said, 'We're just beginning.' Thank you, Mr. Peavler."

Turner said he had numerous influences who were instrumental in his development as an outfielder and as a hitter.

"My Twilight League coach (in Danville), Chuckie Robinson Sr., made my career," he said. "It was his belief in me that made me the ballplayer I was. I never wanted to let him down. In most cases, I don't think that I ever did."

While playing for the Roosters, Turner came under the tutelage of Randy Skaggs. It was, at times, a rocky relationship.

"Randy Skaggs and I never saw eye-to-eye on things," Turner said. "However, I will have to say that he is one of the most intelligent coaches that I have ever played for. I learned an awful lot by listening to his in-game strategies. I never told him how much I respected his coaching ability. I can only hope that during my time with the Roosters he enjoyed the way I approached the game."

Turner was the Roosters' Most Valuable Player in 1985 and a two-time All-Star. He set the Roosters' record for consecutive hits with eight.

"I was a student of the game," he said. "I studied the opposing pitchers and hitters before each game. In many cases, I was already positioned before the ball was even hit due to knowing hitter tendencies. I took away what many thought were going to be hits, especially balls that were driven in the power alleys at Danville Stadium."

Turner experienced some tumultuous times in Danville even before learning that the Roosters wanted to carry on without him.

"It is my personal opinion that Frank Roose (general manager) really didn't care for me," Turner said. "I felt that playing in front of Frank Roose was a continuous audition. As I look back, I feel that audition went fairly well. On the other hand, P.A. announcer Frank Pitlik was an absolute blast. In the first inning of the game, he pronounced my name K.K. Turner. By the fifth inning, my name would be Kaaaaaaaaay Kaaaaaaaaaay Turrrrrrrrrrrner. He was a big supporter of the team and he wore his feelings on his sleeve. He knew the game; he loved the game and he was a real joy to be around."

As a rule, Turner was less focused on who was pitching than with other factors as he prepared to bat.

"My only concern was about the particular pitches that the pitcher was getting over the plate on that day and what the umpire was calling," Turner said. "However, two guys did make me think."

Left-hander Kevin Sprau, from Thomasboro, and right-hander Eric LaVoie, from Buckley, were worthy adversaries.

"Sprau was Mr. Rosin Bag," Turner said. "He would cake that rosin in his hand and the ball would come out of a puff of smoke. This made things very difficult for obvious reasons. Many Roosters complained about him doing this, but hey, whatever works.

Kevin Sprau   Eric LaVoie

"LaVoie had great arm speed on his off-speed pitches. I could never consistently hit his slider. For me, he was just hard to pick up."

As for position players, Turner said two teammates and two opposing players were the ones for whom he developed the greatest respect.

The teammates were Steve Darnell and Mike Johnson.

"Mike was probably one of the best pure hitters that I have had the opportunity to play with," Turner said. "To this day, I have no idea how he hit out of a crouch position. Amazing.

"Stevie was probably the best second baseman in the Midwest. He was never out of position and could turn two as quickly as anyone in the major leagues. He was an excellent situational hitter; very smart on the base paths and rarely, if ever, made base running mistakes."

Thomasboro center fielder Jeff Demith and Rantoul catcher C.R. Black were among the opponents that most impressed Turner. Black and Turner wound up as teammates at Rantoul.

"If you were having a down day, C.R. always had something to say that would put things into perspective," Turner said. "During my years with the Rantoul E.I. team, he was the person that really kept me grounded. Above all, he was a great person and a great catcher.

C.R. Black

"Demo was one of the best opposing hitters I've ever had the opportunity to play against. If the game was on the line, I did not want to see Jeff coming to the plate. Many of my Rooster teammates felt the same way regarding his ability to put the bat on the ball."

Turner and his wife, Teresa, have two daughters. He works in advertising for the Rantoul Press. Though baseball was his sport of choice in college, Turner concedes that he doesn't see many games anymore.

"I don't watch much baseball any more," he said. "PEDs have ruined the game for me."

Scott Rafferty

There are E.I. lifers, such as Gifford-Flatville's Ralph Loschen and Dick Franzen, whose dedication to the league ran the gamut of roles from player to coach to ballpark owner.

Catcher Scott Rafferty showed his own version of dedication.

After graduating from Ball State University, the former Champaign Central standout made weekly commutes from Cincinnati to continue playing for Gifford-Flatville and teams managed by Loschen and Franzen.

Former Gifford-Flatville catcher Scott Rafferty, left, and former Champaign Eagles pitcher Ernie Westfield, formed a battery in an Old-Timers game in 1994 at Rantoul.

"The question has been posed to me several times," Rafferty said. "Why would anybody drive 460 miles round trip every weekend in the summer just to play baseball? I did that for three years. Every Friday afternoon from May to August, I left my job in Cincinnati and headed west to Champaign. As I drove my '71 Chevy Impala down Interstate 74, I was filled with great excitement and anticipation. I couldn't think of any other way I would want to spend my weekend than with my buddies playing baseball."

Rafferty also played for the Giflats for three summers prior to relocating to Cincinnati.

Among the reasons for his commitment to returning were Loschen and Franzen.

"It all started with our coaches," Rafferty said. "They made everything about playing for Gifford fun. We even enjoyed going to practice. They assembled a great team each year."

Though he now lives in suburban Chicago and works for Citadel, Rafferty remains close to many of his former teammates.

"Many of the friendships I made during my years playing for the Giflats continue to this day," he said. "I loved the camaraderie on my Gifford-Flatville teams. I felt very fortunate to play with such a talented and great group of guys."

The nucleus of those Giflat teams included Mike Scholz ("the best pitcher I've ever been on a field with," Rafferty said), Jan South, who grew up in the same neighborhood as Rafferty, Gary Buhr, Renard Danenhower, Richard Franzen, Greg Garland, Bob Harold, Norlyn Loschen, Paul Marsillo, Mike Nichols, Paul Pierce, Dale Schweighart, Mike Seibold, Jack Smith, Dave Strang, Howie Walker,

Ken Warmbier and John Widdersheim.

Rafferty said the bonds formed often included players from opposing teams.

"Make no mistake, we wanted to win every game and the competition was fierce, but at the end of the game, all of the rivalry stuff was left on the field," he said.

As a catcher involved with every pitch, Rafferty was a target for hecklers and rabble-rousers.

"Some of the taunts were actually funny," he said. "Some cannot be printed, but one of my favorites was, 'Pearl Drops,' after the toothpaste. The loyal fans — on both sides of the diamond — added to the atmosphere and made the games more fun."

Following the 1983 season, Rafferty decided to retire.

"Nothing lasts forever. The commute was just getting to be too tough," he said. "Also, given that I was unable to practice during the week, it was getting harder to play at the level I was accustomed to playing."

Rafferty's parents — both of whom have passed away — rarely got to see him play at Ball State, but they had followed his career from Little League to Babe Ruth to Champaign Central to American Legion to Parkland College and were regulars again when he played for the Giflats.

"It always made me feel bad they were unable to watch me play at Ball State, but I got a certain degree of satisfaction knowing that for three additional years they got to watch me play baseball," he said.

Another prime example of a player driven to succeed.

Scott Siddens

Like so many other current and former E.I. All-Stars, the right-handed pitcher was carrying on a family tradition as well as trying to enhance his own career when he first donned an E.I. uniform.

Siddens knew the reputation of the league from his father Robert Siddens, a former E.I. player, and his uncle Ted Siddens, who both played and managed in Rantoul.

"I would listen to the stories of their playing days in the early years of the E.I. League in and around Champaign County," Scott Siddens said. "Hearing stories of games between Rantoul, Gifford-Flatville, Buckley, Royal, etc., at family get-togethers was just a way of life during my pre-teen and teenage years."

So, too, was playing baseball. Growing up in Mattoon, Siddens participated in the sport that has sent more Mattoon athletes on to collegiate careers than any other during the past three decades.

Umpire Fred Strubhar, left, talks with Champaign manager Jack Phillips.

"I was a product of an extensive community-based program for youth that had a rich tradition in mentoring young men in the game," Siddens said, referring to Mattoon's status as a "Baseball Factory" community.

He pitched at both Lake Land Community College and Western Illinois

Catching Up

University and found the competition in the E.I. to be to his liking and exactly what he needed during his off season.

"Summer league play was an important requirement for staying in shape and staying sharp in the game," he said. "Many area baseball players played in the league. The availability of the caliber of baseball the E.I. League offered was an attractive option locally instead of going somewhere else in the country to play over the summer months. Good hitters and nasty curveball pitchers were all over the league."

Siddens played for the Mattoon Braves and then for a Champaign team under the direction of Jack Phillips.

"I'm sure my father was very proud to watch his son play in the same league and, many times, on the same field he did as a young man back in the 1940s and '50s," Scott Siddens said.

When Siddens joined the Champaign Merchants he played alongside many athletes who had been his rivals during their prep careers at different Big 12 Conference schools. One of them was Phillips' son, Rob.

"Many of the guys on the team were guys I had studied on how they swing and hit the ball so I could try and strike them out," Siddens said. "Rivals soon became teammates and we put together a good team that year."

Playing for Phillips was a joy.

"He was a fun man to be around," Siddens said. "His love for the game carried over to everyone around him."

Siddens was hitting his prime and approaching his mid-20s when he left the game.

"Responsibilities change and the time necessary to play in the league changed for me after college ended," he said. "My new job as a police officer working the midnight shift ended my playing years."

He never lost his enthusiasm or respect for the E.I.

"I hope that the current and future players of the league never forget that playing in the league is an honor and a privilege that hundreds of young men before them did with honor," he said. "Baseball is more than just a game. Far more."

Steve Darnell

Danville's foray into the league helped enhance its reputation. The Roosters, who were in existence from 1982 to 1989, played their home games at a former minor league ballpark, Danville Stadium.

Second baseman Steve Darnell and his colleagues felt almost like they were in the minors themselves.

Steve Darnell   Frank Roose

"We'd come in regular clothes, dress there and shower there," Darnell said.

The guiding forces behind the team were Frank Roose and Frank Pitlik.

"The best thing that happened to me was Frank Roose," Darnell said. "I never met a person like Frank. And Pitlik, too. They'd go out of their way to treat us like pro players. We never made it far enough to get there, but we were treated like we were everything. You could go to the mall and the little kids looked up to you."

Roose, in particular, funded much of the team's expenses out of his own pockets.

"Frank did whatever he could to make us happy," Darnell said. "They made sure you had food and they gave you gas money to travel. They didn't have money like that. Frank is one of the greatest men I've ever met in my life. Frank and Myrna (his wife), they don't make people like that any more."

The Roosters played an ambitious schedule, often playing on Wednesdays, Thursdays and Fridays in preparation for the weekend E.I. doubleheader.

"We enjoyed it because we all loved baseball," said Darnell, who turned 49 in February of 2010, "but by the time Sunday got there, we were burnt out. We had the hitters, but our pitchers would run out of gas. We were begging for a day off."

If there was one regret, Darnell said it was that the teams he played for didn't fare better in the postseason. The Roosters' best finish was in 1986 when they lost in the tournament title game to Buckley.

"We had the facilities, but the bad part is we never won the championship," he said. "I guess we were the Cubs."

Even during times of success, there was a hard-luck story.

Darnell and Thomasboro's Greg Jones shared the league's 1986 Most Valuable Player award. The trophy went to Darnell.

"When I got home, I sat the trophy down and the man fell off the top," Darnell said.

In a May 1987 game at Gifford, Darnell suffered a knee injury, which doctors said would sideline him for the remainder of the summer. He underwent surgery but rejoined the team two months later and was 2 for 4 in his first game back.

Teammates and friends helped ease Darnell's burden while he was hobbled.

"After I had the surgery, Davey Parker was there and helped me get dressed," Darnell said.

In retrospect, Darnell said he shouldn't have been so anxious to get back in the lineup.

"Because I rushed it, I had to have surgery three more times on that knee," said Darnell, who works construction in Las Vegas.

At the time he retired following the 1987 season, the 27-year-old Darnell had the highest lifetime batting average (.388) of any active player with at least five years of experience.

The toughest pitchers for Darnell were primarily left-handers, he said, listing Thomasboro's Kevin Sprau, Royal's Jerry O'Neill and Tolono's Gail Ring as three of his main adversaries.

"Sprau had a ball that would break into you," Darnell said. "It was unreal and he was a smart pitcher who knew what he was doing. When he was on, you had a hard night.

"O'Neill was about like Sprau. They had the smartness and the finesse and could make you look

Tolono pitcher Gail Ring

Catching Up

like a fool. Gail Ring gave us fits. The lefties gave us fits."

Darnell appreciated the camaraderie that existed in the E.I.

"After the game, there was no hatred," he said. "When it was over and done with, certain places would feed you. Guys would sit around and drink beer."

Though games with Gifford-Flatville were intense, the postgame atmosphere was friendly and welcoming.

"(Co-coaches) Ralph (Loschen) and Dick (Franzen) were two of the nicest men to talk to," Darnell said, "and Gary Buhr (shortstop) was in the top three. He'd sit around and smile and talk to you. It was just a game to him, too. That league had players with character."

Since leaving Danville in 2003, first for Oregon and then for Las Vegas, one part of Darnell remains unchanged.

"Baseball is still my favorite sport and I'm a diehard Cardinal fan," he said.

His favorite memories are still the ones related to his tenure as a second baseman with the Roosters.

"If I could go back and do it again," Darnell said, "I wouldn't change a thing. Everyone gave it their all. We realized what pro players went through. God has blessed me."

John Harshbarger

When family legacies are discussed and compared, it is hard to ignore the contributions of Albert 'Ab' Harshbarger and his son, John.

"My dad (who was born in 1905) played organized baseball before the E.I. existed and continued to play and manage after the league came into existence," John Harshbarger said.

John Harshbarger

Ab Harshbarger's associations included stints with Ivesdale, Sadorus and Seymour, highlighted by directing Ivesdale's 1940 squad to the tournament championship. Jay Flowers, Joe Ganley and Tommy Morris were among the Ivesdale standouts. Ironically, the team's title-game win came against Thomasboro, the team that John Harshbarger would later star for during his pitching days.

John Harshbarger joined Thomasboro following his sophomore season at Parkland, where he played two years before transferring to the University of Illinois.

"I believe my E.I. success helped lead me to signing with the UI," Harshbarger said.

After two productive E.I. seasons, Harshbarger pitched in the St. Louis Cardinals organization in 1978 and 1979.

He was 4-0 in the Rookie League at Johnson City in '78 and earned a promotion to the Class A entry at Gastonia, where he pitched eight innings the remainder of that season, and 19 the following year in five appearances.

In his minor league career, covering 12 games, Harshbarger had a career ERA of 3.13.

An arm injury halted his professional advancement, but Harshbarger returned to central Illinois in 1980 and helped Marty Kirby coach T'boro.

He rarely pitched but relished his role with the team. When T'boro advanced to the 1982 E.I. Tournament championship game, Harshbarger was rewarded with the start.

The following year, it was back to the third base coaching box for the 6-foot-5 Harshbarger. Perhaps the rest was helpful. When called upon again, he was ready.

"When the tournament came around, our main pitcher (Brad White, from Terre Haute, Ind.) didn't show up for the semifinals and Marty threw me at Danville and we shut them out," Harshbarger said. The next week, I pitched again and we beat Gifford-Flatville 2-0 for our first tournament championship."

He returned to the mound full time in '84 but vowed to make it a one-and-done deal.

"I decided to retire because of the arm pain," Harshbarger said.

The following season, Kirby convinced his then-29-year-old ace to return.

"I was experiencing some personal issues (separation and divorce) and Marty talked me out of retirement," Harshbarger said. "I had my best year ever (13-0)."

The Indians captured both the regular season and the tournament crowns.

"T'boro had some of the most dominant teams in E.I. history during the early to late '80s," said Harshbarger, who realized once and for all in 1986 that the wear and tear on his arm was too much.

He made it through the season and said, "I would have played longer if it weren't for the excruciating pain after pitching."

This time, his retirement was permanent.

He looks back on those summer seasons with a special fondness.

"I wouldn't have met my wife (the former Tami Eggers) if it weren't for E.I." he said. "Marty and (teammate) Bill (Elliott) also met their wives because of E.I. I will bet there are lots of E.I. hookups that led to long-lasting relationships."

Harshbarger and Eggers were married in 1989.

Bob Harold

The former Illini pitcher played professionally in the Cincinnati Reds' organization and also worked out with the Baltimore Orioles' Class AAA affiliate, the Rochester Red Wings.

Bob Harold

Upon his release, Harold was somewhat disillusioned and said, "I was kind of stunned and still processing the whole chain of events, when I received a call at my wife's parents' house from Ralph Loschen. I did not think of playing baseball anymore."

Loschen was the co-manager of a Gifford-Flatville team that participated in both the E.I. League as well as the now-defunct Danville Twilight League at Garfield Park.

Believing he could contribute, Harold accepted the invitation.

"I started to experience a whole new community of baseball fans that were passionate about baseball and players who loved the game and competition," Harold said. "It was good baseball with a great atmosphere."

The midweek Twilight League games in Danville were instrumental in the Giflats maintaining their edge for the weekend.

"Playing in Danville helped us stay sharp for the E.I. games," said Mike Scholz, another of the team's dominant pitchers for more than a decade.

Catching Up

Between 1988 and 1995, Harold compiled a 39-23 cumulative record, including a 10-win season in 1990.

When Harold went to the ballpark, he seldom went alone.

"His kids more or less grew up at the ballpark," Loschen said. "We had Miss America there just about every Sunday."

Actually, the Giflats had a future Miss America in attendance. Erika Harold (who went on to earn her law degree from Harvard) didn't win the coveted crown until 2003, years after her father had retired from baseball.

"I have fond memories of hearing the girls yell, 'Strike 'em out, Dad,'" Loschen said.

Bob Harold said part of the appeal was that Sundays were a time for family togetherness.

"Some of my best memories I have are bringing my four children and my wife and having them cheer me on with pompons and their special cheers," he said. "They loved chasing foul balls and collecting quarters so they could go to the concession stand and buy nachos and cheese.

"They would sit up there in the stands all huddled around that container taking turns dipping into the cheese and having a blast."

Bob Harold wasn't the only family member to participate at the Giflats' ballpark.

"My son, Nicholas, being only 5 years old, sang the national anthem before the start of the league championship game," Bob Harold said. "I was so proud of him and everyone seemed to enjoy it."

Harold, who has an interracial marriage, said his whole family was always treated with respect and welcomed at the venues where the Giflats played.

"I was truly surprised at the warm reception that the fans gave my family," he said. "Having a wife of color and children that are multi-racial could have been a problem, playing in predominately small, white communities. But they were treated like everyone else and made to feel like they were part of the family. They were always excited to get ready to go to the games and it made a great family event. I know that from the times they reminisce about those Sunday afternoons and laugh about the things they did."

Ken Crawford

He will be remembered as a former batting champion as well as the last head coach of a Thomasboro program which ranked among the E.I.'s best throughout much of the 1980s and 1990s.

"I still have the equipment," Crawford said. "Batting helmets. Gear. Baseballs."

Crawford flourished as a player, starting his career with Gifford-Flatville and switching to T'boro, where he wound up being the player-manager.

Ken Crawford

"Personally, I never had a problem being motivated to play," he said. "I lived for it."

Not all of his teammates were that way and the stress and worry about whether there'd be enough players to avoid a forfeit — as well as having a baby join the family — led to Crawford's decision to retire following the 2001 season.

"The coaching thing wore on me," he said. "It took a toll. I was more worried whether we'd have a team and I wasn't able to put the time in to keep my hitting stroke going."

When it became clear T'boro would fold, Crawford had offers to play with other teams. His decision, however, had been finalized.

"I didn't want to be hanging on," Crawford said.

When he was an E.I. rookie, Crawford felt fortunate to play for Gifford-Flatville. That meant one less quality pitcher he had to contend with.

"The best pitcher I ever saw was Bob Harold," Crawford said. "He had unbelievable movement. I was coming out of high school (at Centennial) and playing center field. I'd never seen a slider move like that. He had a 12-to-6 curve that was devastating. I was 18 and glad I was on his team."

When Crawford's roommate, pitcher Dave Seifert, left the Giflats to join Thomasboro, Crawford said, "I went with him."

Buckley outfielder Andy Cotner

The Indians produced championship teams and Crawford said that success has a much greater significance than his individual accolades.

"The league has a long legacy and those championship teams mean a lot more," he said. "I'm proud of the fact we won those championships."

Andy Cotner

There's myriad stories about teenagers who made their debuts in the men's E.I. League and found they could hold their own.

Darrin Fletcher is one example, playing for Royal before he ever had a scholarship offer from the University of Illinois. Matt Herges, who has become a workhorse reliever in the majors, was a former E.I. Player of the Week as a third baseman and pitcher with Gifford-Flatville.

And Andy Cotner, a left-handed pitcher who eventually played for Illinois State University, was introduced to E.I. baseball with the Buckley Dutch Masters as a 16-year-old who still attended Centennial High School.

"It was quite a wakeup call," Cotner said. "In high school or American Legion ball, the players brought Gatorade and big-league chew to the

Thomasboro manager Marty Kirby at his day job as a bricklayer.

93   Catching Up

games. In the E.I. league, they brought Marlboros and Budweiser."

Beyond the brews and the smokes was the fact that his teammates were men; some were twice Cotner's age.

"They had wives. Some of their kids were batboys," he said. "They owned farms and houses. They had real jobs to go to on Mondays. They weren't high school or college baseball players. They were high school or college baseball coaches."

There were more than a few nervous moments for Cotner as he tried to emulate the success he had when playing the game with his peers.

"The first (E.I.) game I ever pitched, I had a home run hit off of me by Jeff Demith (the E.I. career hits leader)," Cotner said. "The next pitch I threw cracked the helmet of Bill Elliott (the E.I. career home run leader). I knew I couldn't let it show I was afraid or I would have never made it. Lacing up the spikes and having the opportunity to compete with and against these guys was a huge thrill and taught me to grow up real quick."

Cotner had the good fortune of playing on some outstanding Buckley teams that featured veterans who averaged at least a decade of playing with the franchise.

It made picking the best athletes he played with easier since the majority were fixtures in the lineup year after year:

> Catcher — Jake Krause. "Troy Genzel was a close second," Cotner said, "but Jake was a hitting machine."
> First base — Mark Scheiwe
> Second base — Chris Hawkins
> Shortstop — Trent Eshleman
> Third base — Dave Gibson
> Outfielders — Tim Kemmer, Eric LaVoie and Tommy Waldrop
> Pitchers — Jason Garrelts, Eddie Moore and Kevin Sprau

Eddie Moore

And the best of the best?

"I have never been one to say, 'He played the game the way it's supposed to be played,' because in the end, it's just a game and it's really up to each individual on how they approach the game. However, Tim Kemmer played the game the way I wanted to play it and the way I enjoyed watching it being played. He was unique in the regard that he was great at everything. He didn't have the most power. He wasn't the fastest and didn't have the best arm, but he was capable of beating you with his power, or by singling five times or winning a game with a great catch or throw. He was the best player I ever played with."

Tim Kemmer

The left-handed hitting Kemmer was the league's Player of the Year in 1990 and fashioned a .358 career average in seven seasons.

Cotner rated Krause and LaVoie as the best pure hitters during his tenure with the Dutch Masters, with Scheiwe the most powerful.

Waldrop, however, was another of the do-everything players in the mold of Kemmer.

"He may have been the best defensive player, but more importantly, he was simply the kind of player whose team was going to win most of the time," Cotner said. "He was a stabilizing force who always played hard and always played to win. He was clutch. He was the guy everyone wanted on their team and the guy you hated playing against. Not only was he incredibly confident in his ability, but everyone around him was more confident because he was wearing the same uniform that you were. He never came off as cocky to the opponent and didn't really get into the trash talking that is so prominent in that league."

Buckley pitcher Eddie Moore

As for a series of outstanding individual achievements, Cotner said some of the most memorable were recorded by Sprau during the 1986 tournament.

"Sprau won all three tournament games and pitched every inning of the tournament," Cotner said. "I'm not sure how old he was, but he was in his 15th season in the league. That was the year Buckley broke a long losing streak without a championship (10 years) and turned the corner on putting together the guts of a team that would eventually win multiple titles."

In the 1986 championship game, Kemmer went 5 for 5, Scheiwe had three doubles that drove in five runs and Cotner was, well, less productive.

"I went 0 for 4 with four strikeouts," he said. "I was terrified that they wouldn't want me back the next year."

He did return and became a player who exuded confidence and helped inspire the belief in others.

Teammate Trent Eshleman recalls the 1999 tournament championship game as a prime example.

"In the top of the 10th inning, Paxton scored two runs to take the lead," Eshleman said. "The quote of the century for the Dutch Masters was spoken that day as Cotner led off the bottom of the 10th with a double.

"He turned to the Swedes' second baseman and said, 'Two runs in the top of the inning was the easy part. Getting us out three times in the bottom of the 10th is the hard part.'"

And, in fact, Paxton was unsuccessful in that quest.

Catching Up

A hit by Eshleman drove in Nate Henrichs from second base with the decisive run. "The biggest hit of my career, by the way," said Eshleman, who regards Cotner as a player with few peers during his E.I. career.

"He was the best player I ever played with in regards to raw baseball talent and unflappable concentration leading towards clutch performances," Eshleman said, "and that is said after playing with numerous professionals, including a handful of major leaguers."

As for tales of perseverance, Cotner said few compare to Eddie Moore, a feisty right-handed pitcher who had an auspicious debut.

Moore had pitched in the Chicago Cubs' farm system and, following his release, joined the Dutch Masters. His first game was against Danville, who had a player legendary for his hitting power, Herman Cunningham.

Danville outfielder Herman Cunningham

"Eddie was extremely surprised at the quality of the opponent he was facing," Cotner recalled. "Coming from AA, he probably expected to handle this 'beer league' with no problem.

"Eddie gets the first two strikes on Cunningham. Going for a strikeout, he throws a biting slider that ends up 6 inches off the ground and off the back of the plate.

"Cunningham proceeds to swing. One hand comes off the bat the way it does with some power hitters. That ball lands about 450 feet away. Immediately, Eddie starts strolling to the dugout before the manager has a chance to take him out.

"He said, 'AA was easier than this. I quit.' Eddie said he'd never seen anything like it."

Though Cunningham had belted a prolific one-handed home run, Moore was talked into keeping his uniform and he became a prominent pitcher on Buckley teams that won multiple championships with him as the pitcher. Moore, in fact, went on to earn E.I. Pitcher of the Year recognition.

The 1990s

Matt Herges was a double winner for Gifford-Flatville in an Aug. 18 game at Rantoul. The right-hander struck out 12 and pitched a four-hitter in the opener, a 7-2 Giflats' win. In the nightcap, he was the fourth pitcher summoned and pitched three innings of three-hit relief as G-F rallied for a 9-7 win. The wins were his first two of the season.

Matt Herges   Greg 'Chip' Immke   Chris Hammack   Rick Wyninger

A week later, he collected a memorable third win. He pitched a no-hitter in a 4-0 win against Tolono. Herges also hit a run-scoring double to supply the lone run he would need.

The wildest game of the year took place on Aug. 19 at Buckley. Thomasboro scored five runs in the top of the seventh to take a 14-9 lead. The Dutch Masters, however, came back with a six-run outburst in the bottom of the seventh to secure a 15-14 win. Dave Gibson's two-out hit knocked in the winning run. Steve Ekhoff, who pitched one-third of an inning of relief, picked up the win, his first decision of the season. Ekhoff had pitched in the opener, relieving in the seventh and walking both batters he faced.

Gifford-Flatville, which needed extra innings to subdue Tolono 5-4 in the semifinals, pounded Rantoul 19-8 in the title game on Sept. 3 at Gifford. Brent Vinson was 5 for 6, including a home run, for the Giflats. He knocked in five runs. Greg 'Chip' Immke (4-2) allowed three hits in his seven-inning stint and picked up the win. Immke was followed to the mound by Doug Miller and Dave Seifert.

Mark McElwain had two hits for Rantoul, both of which were home runs.

The Giflats broke Buckley's 2-year-old record for runs scored in a tournament championship game.

In a midseason survey conducted by The News-Gazette of the five league teams, it was learned that 40 different high schools had alumni playing in the league.

The leaders: Champaign Central (9), Centennial (8), Mahomet-Seymour (7), Buckley-Loda (6), Decatur Eisenhower (5), St. Joseph-Ogden (5), Danville (4) and Rantoul (4). As a sidelight, Gifford-Flatville had an outfield on Opening Day that consisted of three Mahomet-Seymour graduates: Chris Hammack in right, Dave Seifert in center and Rick Wyninger in left.

Paxton, whose coach (Tom Scott) resigned following the 1989 season, was not in the league. The Swedes were unable to find a replacement.

1991

The year started with a major restructuring on the E.I. commission. Al Ellsworth resigned on March 13 after a record 26 years as the league president. Treasurer Phil Quinlan also stepped down.

Former Thomasboro player and manager Marty Kirby was the choice of league managers as the new president. Gary Buhr and Paul Moore were also added as new commissioners.

A Philo team, coached by Brian Plotner, was added to the league and started strong, sweeping Rantoul in a doubleheader at Tolono 5-4 and 7-3 to open the season on May 19. Bob Allison and Spencer Hasler had complete-game pitching performances for Philo.

The remainder of the season didn't go as smoothly. Philo lost its next 21 games. At season's end, it withdrew from the league.

One of the year's most powerful performances was turned in by Gifford-Flatville leadoff batter Chris Hammack in a July 7 game at Tolono. In the opening game of a doubleheader, he was 4 for 5. All four hits were home runs. The right fielder helped the Giflats win, 13-9. For the twin bill, Hammack was 6 for 10.

Dave Allen

1991 All-Stars:
    Catcher, Jason Cavanaugh, Tolono
    First base, Mark Scheiwe, Buckley
    Second base, Dave Allen, Gifford-Flatville
    Shortstop, Mike Dokey, Tolono
    Third base, Dave Gibson, Buckley
    Outfield, Ken Crawford, Gifford-Flatville
    Outfield, Chris Hammack, Gifford-Flatville
    Outfield, Tim Walsh, Thomasboro
    Designated hitter, Bob Mutnansky, Gifford-Flatville
    Utility, Brent Vinson, Gifford-Flatville
    Pitcher, Bob Harold, Gifford-Flatville
    Pitcher, Mike Walling, Buckley

Postseason All-Stars jockey for position. At left is Buckley's Dave Gibson and at right is Paxton's Mike Walling.

In the tournament championship game on Aug. 25 Trent Eshleman hit his first career home run as Buckley dispatched Gifford-Flatville 6-2 in the seventh game of the year between the rivals. Buckley won the series 5-2. The Giflats' final record (21-5) indicates it won every game it played against opponents other than Buckley. The winning pitcher was Jeff Sobkoviak, who had 14 $^1/_3$ scoreless innings in the postseason and was chosen the tournament's Most Valuable Player. For the year, he was 5-1.

Retiring at season's end was Buckley's veteran infielder Scott Lockhart, who ranks sixth all-time for career hits (374).

Buckley's starting lineup in the tourney title game:
    Catcher, Troy Genzel
    First base, Mark Scheiwe

Second base, Chris Hawkins
Shortstop, Trent Eshleman
Third base, Scott Lockhart
Left field, Mike Zuccolo
Center field, Tom Waldrop
Right field, Dave Gibson
Designated hitter, Mike Walling
Pitcher, Jeff Sobkoviak

Scott Lockhart, left, tags a Rantoul runner.

1992

Thomasboro's Mark Dressen, who had pitched just two innings during the final month, was the Indians' postseason catalyst. He pitched 15 consecutive scoreless innings to start the postseason and was the winner in both games as T'boro dispatched Paxton 10-0 in the semifinals and Buckley 9-1 in the title game on Sept. 6. Dressen allowed 12 hits in the two games and one run in 18 postseason innings.

Andy Small and Paul Pierce homered in the finals. Small, Greg Jones, Mike Ruth and Tim Walsh all had two hits against the Dutch Masters. In the semifinals, Jeff Demith was 4 for 5 and Bill Elliott was 3 for 5.

T'boro had opened the season with 15 consecutive wins.

Paxton rejoined the league after a two-year absence. Another newcomer was the Champaign-Urbana Dodgers, whose 20-player roster featured 19 athletes who had played collegiately during the spring. The team played its home games at Parkland College.

In its opening doubleheader, C-U swept Rantoul 12-2 and 6-1. Jamie Sailors pitched a four-hitter and struck out 11 in the Dodgers' first game.

C-U, 16-8 overall, advanced to the semifinals of the postseason tournament after placing third in the regular season.

In an Aug. 8 game at Rantoul, Gifford-Flatville's Brent Vinson swung at a pitch when Thomasboro was trying to issue an intentional walk in the top of the seventh inning. His single drove in Jeff Melecosky with the tying run in a game G-F rallied to win 9-7 in nine innings

Managers:
    Buckley, Scott Lockhart and Mark Scheiwe
    Champaign-Urbana, Dave Johnson and Rod Lovett
    Gifford-Flatville, Joe Lamb and Ralph Loschen
    Paxton, Mark Coplea and Paul Lindauer
    Rantoul, Adam Johnson and Buz Robinson
    Thomasboro, Jeff Corley
    Tolono, Mike Ganley
Commissioners:
    Marty Kirby, President
    Wes Hethke, Secretary
    Gary Buhr, Treasurer

Norm Maier
Paul Moore

1993

For the third time in six years, a different member of the William Paul family was in charge of an E.I. team. Mark Paul, 36, took over at Tolono, following in the footsteps of brothers Tom (Tolono's manager in 1988 and '89) and Stan (Rantoul's manager in 1990).

William Paul was a former coach with the Champaign Knights and Mark Paul said, "I was a batboy even before I went to school."

1993 All-Stars:

Catcher, Brad Allen, Gifford-Flatville
First base, Bill Elliott, Thomasboro
Second base, Kerry Cheely, Champaign-Urbana
Shortstop, Mike Dokey, Gifford-Flatville
Third base, Jon Marchakitus, Rantoul
Outfield, Ken Crawford, Thomasboro
Outfield, Jeff Demith, Thomasboro
Outfield, Jeff Spisok, Gifford-Flatville
Designated hitter, Jake Krause, Buckley
Utility, Jeff Melecosky, Gifford-Flatville
Pitcher, Bob Harold, Gifford-Flatville
Pitcher, Keith Toriani, Thomasboro

Harold (9-1 record, 1.44 ERA) was chosen as the Pitcher of the Year and Toriani (.413 hitter and 8-2 record with 1.77 ERA) was chosen as Player of the Year.

In an Aug. 14 Old-Timers Game at Rantoul, 25 former players participated in a five-inning contest which ended in a 3-3 tie. The oldest player was Dill Seymour, 86, who batted twice and made contact both times. The oldest players to get hits were Ralph Loschen, 68, and Al Ellsworth, 67.

In the tournament championship game on Sept. 5 at Gifford, Thomasboro's Keith Toriani earned the win as the Indians defeated Gifford-Flatville 9-7. He also slugged two home runs as well as pitching his third consecutive complete game in the postseason.

Coach Jeff Corley's starting lineup in the final game:

Catcher, Paul Pierce
First base, Bill Elliott
Second base, Bill Wantland
Shortstop, Brad Wagers
Third base, Trent Wagers
Left field, Gene Simmons
Center field, Jeff Demith
Right field, Chris Davis
Pitcher, Keith Toriani

Paul
Pierce

1994

During a championship game in which the teams combined for seven home runs, Charleston-Mattoon handed Thomasboro an 11-7 setback on Sept. 4 at Rantoul.

The winners joined the league in 1993 and played on the road in both the semi-finals and finals, overcoming deficits each week.

Scott Albright's fifth-inning single drove in Steve Otto with the run that put C-M ahead to stay, 5-4. Rick Royer had three hits for Charleston-Mattoon. Thomasboro's Jeff Demith hit two home runs.

In the semifinals, Charleston-Mattoon upset top-seeded Buckley 9-8.

During a regular season game in July, Pitcher of the Year Bob Harold celebrated his 40th birthday with a 1-0, three-hit shutout against Buckley.

In a July 4 doubleheader at Rantoul, T'boro's Ken Crawford supplied the fireworks. He was 7 for 10 (three home runs) and drove in 11 runs.

Managers:
    Buckley, Mark Scheiwe
    Charleston-Mattoon, Ed Buxton
    Gifford-Flatville, Hans Flessner, Dick Franzen and Ralph Loschen
    Paxton, Paul Lindauer
    Rantoul, Jason Campbell and Donnie Fitzgarrald
    Royal, Rick Phillips and Buddy Kuhstoss
    Thomasboro, Jeff Corley

Hans Flessner

1995

Thomasboro's Ken Crawford, a year out of the University of Illinois, broke the 48-year-old single-single batting record, registering 37 hits in 68 at-bats for a .544 average. The previous mark, .538, was set by Buckley's Carl Wolf in 1947. In the tournament finals, Thomasboro and Keith Toriani topped Buckley 7-5.

1995 All-Stars:
    Catcher, Jake Krause, Buckley
    First base, Bill Elliott, Thomasboro
    Second base, Bill Wantland, Thomasboro
    Shortstop, Braden Gibbs, Paxton
    Third base, T.J. Posey, Buckley
    Outfield, Brad Cosgrove, Paxton
    Outfield, Jeff Demith, Thomasboro
    Outfield, Chad Isley, Charleston-Mattoon
    Designated Hitter, Nick Riddle, Rantoul
    Utility, Mark Coplea, Paxton,
    Pitcher, Steve Ekhoff, Buckley
    Pitcher, Brett Robinson, Gifford-Flatville
    Player of the Year, Ken Crawford, Thomasboro

Managers:
    Buckley, Mark Scheiwe and Virgil Scheiwe
    Charleston-Mattoon, Rob Brown and Terry McDevitt
    Gifford-Flatville, Hans Flessner, Bob Harold and Ralph Loschen
    Paxton, Mark Coplea and Jeff Graham
    Rantoul, Jason Campbell and Scott Deaville

Thomasboro, Jeff Corley and Jeff Demith
Commissioners:
Marty Kirby, President
Dave Strang, Treasurer
John Harshbarger
Wes Hethke
Paul Moore

1996

Buckley outfielder Tom Waldrop collected 31 hits in 55 at-bats and his .563 batting average shattered the all-time single-season record, which had stood for one season. He was also the league's toughest batter to strikeout, fanning on just .033 percent of his plate appearances.

Tournament champion Charleston-Mattoon had a tough path to the title. It had to beat the second and first seeds in road games. In the finals, C-M topped Thomasboro 13-5.

1996 All-Stars:
Catcher, Jake Krause, Buckley
First base, Rob Brown, Charleston-Mattoon
Second base, Brad Cosgrove, Paxton
Shortstop, Terry McDevitt, Charleston-Mattoon
Third base, T.J. Posey, Buckley
Outfield, Andy Cotner, Buckley
Outfield, Ken Crawford, Thomasboro
Outfield, Chad Isley, Charleston-Mattoon
Outfield, Tom Waldrop, Buckley
Designated hitter, Nick Riddle, Rantoul
Utility, Clint Benhoff, Crawford County
Pitcher, Steve Ekhoff, Buckley
Pitcher, Brad Wagers, Thomasboro

Andy
Cotner

1997

Buckley followed its regular season crown by securing the tournament championship. The Dutch Masters defeated Gifford-Flatville 11-6.

Managers:
Buckley, Mark Scheiwe and Virgil Scheiwe
Charleston-Mattoon, Robert Brown and Ken Coffey
Crawford County, Steve Atwood and Steve Sheets
Gifford-Flatville, Richard Franzen and Norlyn Loschen
Paxton, Brad Cosgrove and Jason Ronna
Rantoul, Jason Campbell and Scott Deaville
Thomasboro, Jeff Demith and Les Little
Tolono, John Radmaker and Roy Radmaker
Commissioners:
Marty Kirby, President
John Harshbarger, Secretary

Dave Strang, Treasurer
Paul Moore

1998

Blake Winemiller's 11th win of the season enabled Thomasboro to post an 8-7 win against Paxton in the tournament title game. Josh Shelmadine earned the save. Chris Davis and Scott Scharlau hammered homers for T'boro. Teammates with two hits were Ken Crawford, Kyle Kimme and Brian Reed.

Jeff Demith, 35, had a run-scoring double, helping T'boro to the tournament title for the seventh time in the nine championship games in which he played. Demith retired as a full-time player at season's end but played briefly each of the next two seasons, batting 40 more times.

1999

Paxton scored twice in the top of the 10th inning to snap a 5-5 tie in the tournament championship game, but Buckley rebounded with three runs in the bottom of the inning for an 8-7 conquest. P.J. Moore (5-0) picked up the win, striking out six in three innings of relief. Jake Krause and Nate Henrichs each had two hits for the Dutch Masters.

Trent Eshleman's two-strike, two-out, opposite-field single to right drove in Kurt Krumwiede with the tying run and Nate Henrichs with the game-winner.

For Paxton, Mark Prina had three hits and Chad Rock drove in three runs.

In their season series, Buckley held a 5-1 edge, but four of the wins were by one run and three of the contests required extra innings.

Buckley's Trent Eshleman makes a throw.

There was a marked contrast in the makeup of the teams. Paxton started eight players in the semifinals who had played either in college or high school in the spring. For Buckley, the average age of its starters was over 30, including shortstop Terry McDevitt, 35, who commuted weekly from Chatham.

McDevitt was the E.I.'s regular season Most Valuable Player. He was one of three veterans who retired at game's end, joining Troy Genzel and Dave Gibson.

Buckley's starting lineup:
Catcher, Jake Krause
First base, Todd Post
Second base, Chris Hawkins
Shortstop, Terry McDevitt
Third base, Trent Eshleman
Left field, Nate Henrichs
Center field, Brian Naese
Right field, T.J. Posey
Designated hitter, Mark Scheiwe

Mark
Scheiwe

Pitcher, Jake Zajc
Managers:
    Buckley, Mark Scheiwe and Virgil Scheiwe
    Crawford County, Garett Graham and Tony Graham
    Danville, Frank Atwood and Mike High
    Gifford-Flatville, Richard Franzen and Norlyn Loschen
    Paxton, Brad Cosgrove and Jason Ronna
    Rantoul, Jason Campbell and Scott Deaville
    Thomasboro, Ken Crawford and Les Little
    Tolono, John Radmaker and Roy Radmaker
Commissioners:
    Marty Kirby, President
    John Harshbarger, Secretary
    Les Hoveln
    Louie Krumwiede
    Paul Moore

Stars of the 1990s

Marty Kirby

The Urbana native is one of the few individuals who've run the gamut of roles in the E.I. League. He started out as a fan, then became a player and followed that up with a successful managerial career. He capped off his tenure by serving as the E.I. president.

Kirby said he couldn't help but notice the league as a teenager.

"E.I. baseball was plastered all over the paper every Monday," he said. "Front-page articles in sports, and pictures. The *Champaign-Urbana Courier* was still alive (until 1979), so you could read the double coverage (along with what was reported in the *Champaign-Urbana News-Gazette*). E.W. Hesse was the E.I. guru. He had a great interest in baseball, and it showed in his reporting. I worked my hardest to make sure I was good enough to make the Monday headlines in a league that I had never watched a game."

Kirby and his childhood buddy, Randy Halberstadt, had a well-established start in the summertime sport.

"I met Randy when I was 12 years old," Kirby said. "Little League baseball was at its strongest (in Champaign-Urbana). I played for Sunbeam Bread in the Yankee Ridge League (on a team coached by his father, Merwin). Halby played for Coca-Cola in the Southern League (on a team coached by his father, Ralph Sr.)"

At season's end, they became teammates on an all-star team (the Champaign-Urbana Blues) that won five of the six tournaments it entered. A left-hander, Kirby pitched six no-hitters that summer in the 11-12-year-old league.

More importantly, a passion had been borne that would last for decades.

"I was in love with the greatest sport on the face of the earth," Kirby said.

In 1973, Kirby and Halberstadt were teammates on an Urbana High School team that won the Big 12 championship (which has not happened again through the 2010 season).

They remained teammates on Urbana's American Legion Post 71 team and planned to be on the Gifford-Flatville E.I. roster.

"It was the most exciting baseball news I had ever had," Kirby said.

The feeling was short lived, however. Two weeks before the season started, "Gifford-Flatville rescinded the offer," Kirby said. "Little did I know that this would be the beginning of a very interesting journey over the next nine years. When complete, it turned out to be the best time of my life."

Halberstadt, a second baseman, joined the Royal Giants where another former Urbana athlete (John Hiser) had played the previous year. Kirby, primarily an outfielder and first baseman, settled on Tolono.

"I had the Tolono uniform in my possession for 3 hours and Royal called, offering a spot on the roster." Kirby said. "Talk about bittersweet. I had not even played a game, and this E.I. League was not very fun."

He was torn about whether to join the buddies he'd known for years or honor the commitment he'd made to Tolono.

"I told my dad, and I knew what his response would be before he offered it," Kirby said. "He said, 'You made a commitment to a manager and a team. If you are going to change your decision, call him, meet with him and explain to him what happened.'"

Kirby made a followup trip to Tolono to return the uniform.

"The manager was disappointed, but respectful of what I told him," Kirby said. "I felt terrible driving back home."

Kirby didn't regret the decision.

"The people of Royal were amazing baseball fans and great people," he said. "Harper Park has been long gone, like Chief Illiniwek at the University of Illinois. If you ever played at Harper Park, you will never forget it. Like one dance of the Chief, it is tattooed in your soul for life."

Though Kirby was the Giants' fourth outfielder and received limited playing time, he said, "I made some good friends I still see. One in particular is Herb Osterbur. He is a true ambassador of the E.I. League and there is not enough room to honor him."

If there were thoughts of leaving the team, then Kirby put those aside as he recalled one of his father's mantras.

"Dad's mission statement was, 'Attitude is everything,'" Kirby said. "I live by that statement every day and, amazingly, so do my four children."

Halberstadt and Kirby both played collegiately at Parkland College, where they had the good fortune to come under Jim Reed's tutelage.

"I learned more about baseball from Coach Reed than from anyone before or after," Kirby said.

His two-year stint with the Cobras was followed by two years at the University of Illinois.

Kirby's summers remained filled with baseball.

"One summer, I played in three leagues, the E.I., the Danville Twilight League and the CICL," he said. "Sometimes it was eight games a week. I would work all day, travel two hours if we were on the road and make the return trip, arriving home at 1 or 2 a.m. I loved it."

In particular, being a member of the Danville Roosters was a memorable experience.

"For the first time, I saw kids begging for autographs on a team I was playing on," he said. "The players were from all over the country. We had a 13-man roster and in the coming years nine were drafted."

Kirby was not one of them, but he was satisfied with his situation.

"Sunday afternoon baseball in the E.I. League topped everything," he said.

After one year at Royal, Kirby hooked up with a rebuilding Thomasboro program that was coming off a sub-.500 season.

"They were looking for a package deal of players," said Kirby, who was one of the first to be recruited by the Indians.

Once he was in the fold, Thomasboro manager Norm Maier asked his opinion on other players who could help make the team immediately competitive.

"Even though I didn't know it, by selecting other players, it would be the start of seeing that I was destined to coach," Kirby said.

His efforts helped T'boro quickly turn around its fortunes.

"They already had Bob McCartney, Jeff Corley and Mark Salisbury," Kirby said. "When it was done, I talked John Harshbarger, Randy Halberstadt, Don Skorup and Tom Gaige" into joining.

In the summer of 1976, Thomasboro won 17 games, but Kirby said, "more importantly, it opened a pipeline (with Parkland College) that would provide more talent than you could ever imagine."

A winning season had a major impact at the gate, as well.

"The fan base went from average to unbelievable," Kirby said. "We were still not on the level of the Giflats or Buckley, but we were headed in that direction."

The progression continued through the summer of 1979. Kirby was a fixture in the lineup. As plans were being made for 1980, Maier announced that he would step aside as the manager.

Thomasboro manager Marty Kirby

"Everyone, including me, was wondering who would be our new manager. Out of nowhere," he said, the answer came. "I was asked to manage the 1980 Thomasboro Indians."

It was a daunting proposition for a 24-year-old who said, "I was in the prime of my playing career and loving every second of it."

If he accepted, he would be surrounded by "teammates who were older than me."

He said, "no."

Actually, Kirby was more emphatic. "NO!" he said.

"I wanted to play and win an E.I. batting title while leading T'boro to an E.I. championship," he said.

Kirby soon felt backed into a corner. Not only did the upper-level team management want him to be in charge, but so too did the majority of the players.

"The players lobbied me and offered total support," Kirby said. "Many stated that if one of the assistants were promoted, they weren't coming back. We were on the verge of being a contender and they were bailing if I didn't take over. I was mad and flattered at the same moment."

The offer was subsequently sweetened. Kirby could be a player-manager.

"I reluctantly said yes," he said. "Deep inside my competitive baseball soul I knew this would probably hurt me on a player level, but I didn't want the dream of winning an E.I. title to disappear."

All around, Kirby received a warm welcome.

"The fans of T'boro embraced me," Kirby said. "We had special cookouts every Sunday. We had lots and lots of fans, many I am still great friends with to this day. Reflecting back, I could not have done it without them. I was the perfect fit for what we both wanted: the E.I. championship."

And then it happened.

Not once, not twice. Not even a threepeat. The championships in 1982, 1983 (shared), 1984 and 1985 were historical in their significance.

"It was the first time any team had won or shared an E.I. (regular season) championship four years in a row," Kirby said. "A team that had won two games just a few years before was establishing a small dynasty."

Thomasboro's 1982 team showed the depth of the relationship with Parkland College. Every squad member that season, except one, had attended Parkland.

His mission completed, Kirby retired from coaching (and occasionally playing) following the 1985 season. He left following what he called "probably the best baseball team I ever managed," a squad anchored by right-handed pitcher John Harshbarger, whose season record was 13-0, including postseason play.

Kirby's decision was based on more than the desire to go out as a winner and with a legacy that would last for years.

At an E.I. game, he had met his future wife, Tammie Widloski. They set September of 1986 as their wedding date.

Kirby had no intention of entering a new phase of his life with outside obligations.

"My commitment to her would be as strong as it was to baseball," Kirby said. "I was fine with that. I was 30 and wanting a family."

Within a few years, the Kirbys had four children. The first came in 1987 and the last two arrived in February of 1990, as a package deal: twins Mandy and Megan Kirby.

The E.I. League did not become a long-lost memory. Kirby was hand picked by former E.I. president Al Ellsworth to be his successor.

"I was honored and accepted," Kirby said, "as it would get me back in the league without the total commitment."

For years, Ellsworth had been one of Kirby's role models.

"He was a man of great honesty and fairness," Kirby said. "I always admired the way he ran the league. As great as the E.I. League is, his name is bigger than all others together."

Kirby's return coincided with various changes within the league. The traditional Mother's Day weekend start to Labor Day weekend conclusion would soon be revised. The number of teams would fluctuate, though Kirby was adamant not to turn anyone away.

"There was no trimming," he said. "If a team was there (at the preseason organizational meeting) and could field a team, they were in. The perfect league at that time was eight teams, but it is difficult to get exactly the number of teams you want. One year we had seven, the next nine."

Soon after overseeing a revision in the bylaws (1999) — the first overhaul since 1985 — Kirby relinquished control as his children grew and he found himself back in a coaching capacity.

He devoted 15 more years coaching various youth-league teams and had what he considered a remarkable accomplishment.

"In those years, I had one problem with one parent," Kirby said. "Later that parent came by my house and apologized and admitted he was wrong. Attendance at my practices was 100 percent. These are probably my greatest coaching wins."

Like those who have come before him — and those who will follow — vivid recollections are etched into the permanent memory bank. One story Kirby retains helps to illustrate the passion that exists for the league.

Kirby and Harshbarger — at a time when both were commissioners — were taking the gate at a championship game at Buckley.

"One of the greatest names in E.I. history, Rodell Gerdes, walks up to John and me and proceeds to tell John he hit a home run off of him," Kirby said. "John's response was classic: 'Yeah, everyone that batted against me hit a home run off of me.'

"Rodell then removes his wallet and takes out a clipped-out newspaper article that proved his statement. Rodell had not played in a game in 15 years. I laughed until I had tears running down my face, thankful that another E.I. memory lives."

T.J. Posey

For T.J. Posey, Sunday afternoon doubleheaders were never viewed as relaxing moments with washed-up players.

It was a serious venture. "It was not a Sunday beer league," Posey said. "Sunday afternoons were strictly business."

He played at a high level for years and was a starter for a men's basketball team at Illinois Wesleyan University that reached the Final Four, but even those experiences didn't prepare him for what he faced in the E.I.

"I can honestly say that the butterflies may have been worse playing Gifford-Flatville, Thomasboro or Paxton in an E.I. championship game," Posey said.

"It was like Trent Eshleman would tell all of the college baseball players that would start the season with us, 'You may pitch on a college team and someday play Division I baseball, but you will never face the pressure that you have in Buckley on a Sunday afternoon playing for the Dutch Masters.'"

The expectations, Posey said, extended beyond a successful outcome on the field.

"They expect you to win with class, carry yourself with pride and leave everything on the field," Posey said. "Anything less was considered disheartening."

Ultimately, Posey's attitude about a season was based on whether Buckley won or lost in the postseason tournament.

"I remember losing championship games to T'boro and to Paxton and just being devastated the entire winter," he said.

Buckley fans had high expectations for Posey when he joined the Dutch Masters in 1993. His father, Tom, had started his decade-long career with Buckley in 1974 and twice won league batting titles prior to his retirement.

T.J. Posey accompanied his family to the weekly games but was too young — or too involved chasing foul balls — to retain many memories about how his father played.

"I probably learned more about his game from guys like Ken Johnson (who coached Buckley from 1993 to 2005) and Mark Scheiwe (a teammate of both Poseys)," T.J. Posey said.

The late Bill Wolf saw similarities in the father-son duo.

"'You hit to right-center, just like your old man,' was a phrase used by Billy Wolf, who watched me go from a toddler to a Dutch Master," T.J. Posey said.

The young Posey came close to duplicating his father's feat as a batting champion. His unsuccessful bid in 2005, he said, can be blamed on no one but himself.

"The final weekend, I decided to stay out late on a Saturday night until the early hours of Sunday morning at some wedding reception and went 0 for 8 that next day," T.J. Posey said. "Those late Saturday nights had an effect on a number of Dutch Masters' performances throughout those years, probably more for the worse than the better."

One common thread on many of the Buckley teams for which T.J. Posey played was the number of teammates who were coaches, either for high schools or summer teams. In addition to Posey, who coached at Iroquois West (and subsequently played with several of those athletes on the Dutch Masters, such as Kyle Leydens, Brock Niebuhr and Nick Runyon), other coaches included Eshleman, Scheiwe, Steve Ekhoff, Chris Hawkins, Jake Krause and Todd Post.

Having that nucleus together on game day was an asset, Posey said, because "most of us had a strong desire to succeed."

When Posey enrolled at Illinois Wesleyan, after his graduation from Prairie Central, his focus was strictly on basketball.

"I did not have a strong interest to playing baseball at that time," he said.

Being with the Dutch Masters as a rookie in 1993 prompted an attitude adjustment.

"I remember going back to Wesleyan wanting to play baseball as well as basketball," he said. "I learned more about baseball that one summer than I had my entire life."

His 13-year playing career in the E.I. would likely have been longer, Posey said, had he and his wife not relocated to southern Illinois. He now teaches and coaches at Belleville East High School. One season making the three-hour one-way commutes was enough.

The '05 Dutch Masters swept the regular-season and tournament crowns and an elated Posey said, "I would want to end it no other way."

Return visits to Buckley's ballpark always bring to mind a comment from former teammate Eshleman, words which Posey finds are even more valid now that he has been away for a while.

"When one looks around as they enter the baseball premises in Buckley, they understand why it is as Trent Eshleman used to say, 'the center of the universe.'"

The Iroquois County community is not a major metropolitan town. In the 2000 census, Buckley's population was listed as 593 residents.

Mark Scheiwe

Few families have tenures in the E.I. to match the Scheiwes.

It started with Virgil Scheiwe, a renowned pitcher who stayed active after his playing days ended by coaching and then serving on the grounds crew. The field in Buckley was named in his honor during a 1999 ceremony.

His sons, Mark and Phil, both played for the Dutch Masters as did Mark's son Ryne.

From left, Buckley's Scott Garrelts and Mark Scheiwe

When you've grown up around the legacy, it takes something special happening to put it in the proper perspective.

"It didn't hit me until they put the diamond in his name," Mark Scheiwe said.

Mark pitched in his first E.I. game as a 17-year old in 1978 "at Rantoul, against (Thomasboro's) Kevin Sprau," he recalled.

After graduating from Buckley-Loda High School a year later — in the same class as Scott Garrelts — the tiny school had two of its players picked in the 1979 amateur baseball draft.

Garrelts was the 15th player selected in the first round and made it to the majors as a 20-year-old pitcher with the San Francisco Giants. Garrelts played parts of 10 seasons in the majors, eventually compiling a 69-53 record to go with 48 saves.

Mark Scheiwe was also drafted as a pitcher, going to the Chicago Cubs in the 15th round. He played in the minors for parts of three seasons before a shoulder injury prompted his release.

Scheiwe said it wasn't necessarily a surprise that a high school with 175 total students would have two players taken in the same major league draft.

"We didn't have football in school," he said. "Baseball was the main sport."

As a rookie in the Gulf Coast League, Scheiwe was the team's winningest pitcher (4-2 record). A year later, also in the Gulf Coast League, his 3-2 mark was one behind the team leader, but more than future major leaguers Jeff Bair and Randy Martz, who were his teammates.

Buckley first baseman Mark Scheiwe

Though he was raised on the Dutch Masters — "I was the batboy and worked my way up," Scheiwe said — he wasn't keen on playing following his release from the Cubs' organization after two games in 1981 with the Class A affiliate in Quad Cities.

"I went to all the (E.I.) games," Scheiwe said. "My dad talked me into it. I'd been around it all my life, but it was tough. I had my sights set a little higher."

Mark Scheiwe wound up playing or coaching for the Dutch Masters in parts of four decades. One highlight came in 2003, after Trent Eshleman had taken over the managerial duties and Scheiwe thought he had permanently put away his first baseman's mitt.

He was involved in farm work one Sunday when the team found itself short of players for a preseason game.

"Esh called and got me out of the fields," Mark Scheiwe said. "I came in and got to play with Ryne. Playing with my son was fun. I was ready to retire after that."

He had a good farewell sendoff.

"Mark had three hits, including a double that rocketed off the left field wall, and a bunt single," Eshleman said.

Eshleman believes if Scheiwe had been in the Cubs' organization in a different era, his professional career might still have flourished.

"Had Mark been a higher draft pick, you may have seen a situation like Rick Ankiel's where Mark would have become a hitter and position player in pro baseball," Eshleman said. "Mark could hit the ball harder, on a line, than anyone I ever knew. He would hit balls that would either dent the wall or fly over it and make it that distance in a heartbeat. Third basemen had to be scared and many moved back towards the edge of the outfield grass when he approached the plate, especially in the aluminum bat era."

Eshleman said one line best sums up Scheiwe's hitting skills.

"We always said you could sneak a sunrise past a rooster easier than you could sneak a fastball by Scheiwe," he said.

Like his father, Mark Scheiwe found he couldn't totally remove himself from the picture. He continues to help work on the field.

"I go out Sunday mornings and make sure everything's ready," he said. "I enjoy doing it. For a town like Buckley, that's about what everybody lives for. You don't find many teams like that."

Nor do you find many families like the Scheiwes.

While Scheiwe continues to help water and maintain the field, he is joined by a dependable crew of volunteers that also includes Jim Hull, Russ Plath, Del Steinmann, Stan Sheetz and Wilmer Tholen.

As a sidenote, there is no record of Garrelts ever appearing in an E.I. game with Buckley, though he was on the roster and did pitch for the team when it participated in the Danville Twilight League.

Trent Eshleman
In his rookie season in the E.I. League (1990), Eshleman wound up with stronger memories from what occurred away from the park.

A shortstop, he helped the Dutch Masters to a third-place finish in the tournament while playing alongside batting champion Tim Kemmer.

A center fielder, Kemmer's name was etched into the all-time record book for being part of the first (and still only) father-son duo to win batting championships. His father, Butch Kemmer, was the league's top hitter in 1969.

The night young Kemmer received his trophy, Eshleman drove him back to his home in Loda.

Buckley's Trent Eshleman (holding helmet) is congratulated by teammates.

"We were stopped by a train at the north end of Paxton, by the grain elevator," Eshleman said. "I remember Tim saying how he had gotten his life together and had secured a good job. He also mentioned that he and his father were getting along for the first time in some period. Tim had been an extraordinary player in his youth but mentioned that perhaps he had squandered some opportunities both on and off the field. However, things were looking up for him at that time. He was refreshed."

Two weeks later, on Sept. 15, 1990, the 24-year-old Kemmer died in an automobile accident on Route 150 west of Champaign.

"His death shocked the Dutch Master family and was a very difficult time for those who knew him," Eshleman said. "The funeral was gut-wrenching. I had known him for just a very short time but respected him for both his outstanding baseball prowess and for his willingness to right the ship in his life and move forward in a positive way."

Kemmer is buried in St. John's Cemetery, about one-half mile to the east of the center field area he roamed while starring for the Dutch Masters.

"His gravestone has a baseball hitter wearing a cap with a Buckley Dutch Master 'B' on it," Eshleman said, "another reminder of the powerful influence held by the Dutch Master fraternity to those who are, or were, a part of it."

Buckley outfielder Tim Kemmer

Eshleman learned early to tune out comments from the fans, especially those in Paxton who are in the unique position of being part of the same school district (Paxton-Buckley-Loda) during the school year, but bitter rivals from mid-May through Labor Day.

Though the most vociferous fans can be unrelenting, Eshleman appreciates one gesture he has seen.

"I could not begin to share the personal attacks made towards me during my career, but I can share that the Paxton fans that know and love the game communicated respect for good play for me once the final out of a doubleheader was made," Eshleman said.

"The likes of Reuben Shilts and Mike Nuckols would always rib me from atop the third base dugout about my age or my play if I made a mistake, but they always gave me a subtle thumbs up or recognized me in some manner when I did something well on the field, even if it meant their beloved Swedes losing."

The key to a long career, Eshleman contends, is to not get riled by the fans.

"I often tell players who have not experienced such ribbing, you must subscribe to what allowed me to survive for 20 years," Eshleman said, "tuck your ears in and never acknowledge those fans or they will eat you alive. This pressure makes E.I. players better equipped to handle the next level of play."

Paxton Swedes

In 1968, the Paxton Merchants started an association with the E.I. League. Among the ramrods were former Buckley player Bob Nuckols and Carl Hudson Jr., a local druggist who managed and helped fund the venture.

Three years later, the team changed its nickname to the Swedes. The team has endured — with a brief hiatus in the early 1990s — now for more than three decades.

The 1968 season also coincided with the year that Jim 'Crow' Fox graduated from Paxton High School.

"Crow would be considered by many to be the face of the Paxton Swedes," current coach Mark Prina said.

Lonnie Bauer

Fox played or coached for nearly 25 years and continued his affiliation along with his wife, Carol, as the Swedes' financial managers.

By the 1970s, Fox was part of a solid corps of players who helped Paxton become a league fixture.

Among the others who played major roles were shortstop Lonnie Bauer, first baseman Steve Coplea, pitcher Rodell Gerdes, center fielder Jim Golden, shortstop Bobby Larson, second baseman Randy Peterson, infielder Pat Prina and pitcher Bill Snyder.

Decades later, their reputations — and antics — still remain.

"Some think Bauer is the best defensive shortstop ever to play in the E.I.," Mark Prina said.

Snyder, who remains one of the team's most loyal and fervent fans, was known as one of the Swedes' most colorful characters.

Relating stories he heard, Mark Prina said, "he pitched Game 2 because he was never home from the night before in time for Game 1."

Pat Prina, a former University of Iowa player, began teaching in Paxton in 1968, but he didn't play for the Swedes until 1973. His influence would be felt as much for helping develop players as it was for his standout play on the field.

Many of the Swedes who were in uniform in the 1990s and early 2000s were coached by Pat Prina in high school as he developed not only college talent, but also a feeder system of athletes who would return to their hometowns for the summers and help the Swedes soar into a position of prominence.

Paxton's brief departure from the E.I. was due, in part, to baseball being dropped at the high school level in 1977. Young players weren't learning the fundamentals and interest in the game waned.

Kevin Johnson

Still, numerous standouts helped Paxton carry on its summer tradition. Noteworthy contributors included pitchers Darrin Kregel and Mike Walling along with Kevin Johnson, whom Mark Prina called, "one of the best Swedes hitters of all time."

A major resurgence took place in the 1990s. It started at the grassroots level. The Paxton and Buckley-Loda high school districts consolidated in 1991 (two years after they had started a sports co-op) and Pat Prina found a bevy of prospects within the prep teams each spring.

The 1989 Buckley-Loda team had captured a regional championship. Some of the mainstays soon became summer-league standouts: Mark Coplea, Jeff Graham, Brian Martin, Kenny Mutchmore and Jason Stalter among others.

Mark Prina

Coplea and Mutchmore played collegiately at Millikin University, in Decatur, and were responsible for an influx of their college teammates joining the Swedes in the summer.

Behind the scenes, important developments took place. Jason Ronna was a prominent part of the revitalization.

"Jason began taking care of the field (Memorial Field, behind Clare Peterson Elementary School) and sought out the right people to help with major improvements," Mark Prina said.

His groundskeeping duties have continued, and entering 2010, Mark Prina said, "Jason has made it one of the best amateur fields in all of Illinois."

The rebuilding phase of the team reached new heights in 1994 when Southern Illinois University athlete Brad Cosgrove started spending his summers in Paxton and gained commitments from many of his college buddies.

Braden Gibbs, who earned Most Valuable Player honors in the Missouri Valley Conference, and Jamie Sailors (a former Parkland College pitcher who spent time in the St. Louis Cardinals organization) were among the Swedes' key additions.

"The addition of Brad meant that the Swedes would begin getting the outside players needed to complement the local players, a formula we still use today to field one of the best teams in the league every year," Mark Prina said.

PBL High School's regional championship team of 1996 supplied another group of strong players later in the decade, when several of the team's veterans started to step aside.

Chris Jones went from PBL to Millikin and continued that player pipeline.
In 1999, Paxton won the regular-season title and advanced to the tournament's championship game.

A second generation of Swedes accepted management positions as the new millennium started. Pat Prina started a stint as coach with son Mark as a key associate. Corey Fox and Andy Gerdes had expanded roles beyond playing, too, and another Prina son, Jerry, soon joined as well, and was another of the catalysts as Paxton emerged as one of the premier programs of the 2000s.

The Swedes started the new decade by winning the regular season crown in 2000.

Besides being standout players, Mark Prina said the second-generation group made certain they were surrounded by other equally talented athletes.

"More importantly is that we went out and found the major pieces of the puzzle to help the Swedes win championships," Mark Prina said.

An assistant coach at Danville Area Community College, Mark Prina encouraged players from Vermilion County to continue playing in the summer by joining the Swedes. Andy Gerdes, an area umpire, helped locate others who could contribute.

Among the key additions which would help form the nucleus for the successful upcoming teams were Buddy Dubois, J.T. Furnish, Chris Hughes, Luke Humphrey, Scott Lucht, Jonathan Smiley and Dylan Ward.

"Most of these guys were a part of the 2004 championship series, which the Swedes consider their best games in team history," Mark Prina said. "Some even think the Sunday games (of that tournament) were the best doubleheader in E.I. history."

Mark Prina is optimistic that the groundwork has been established so that the program will remain on solid footing even as members of the 2008 and 2009 teams that reached the tournament finals decide to retire.

"Many of the current older players have changed roles as they continue to play," he said. "They not only play at a competitive level still, but they are teaching and passing on knowledge of the game and the league to the younger players. It's a fun time for the Swedes because there are so many older players mixed in with the younger guys."

Players for the future include Dylan Overstreet, a nephew of former Swedes Steve and Mark Coplea, who won't graduate from high school until 2011.

"This creates new excitement for everyone," Mark Prina said. "Usually, there is mass changeover and it takes a couple of years to become competitive again, but there are enough older players still playing that the change isn't so drastic."

One aspect which doesn't change is the commitment from those who have been involved for years. Besides the efforts of the Foxes, former player Rodell Gerdes runs the gate for the home games and helps chase foul balls while Becky Prina is in charge of the concession stand.

"The one word which best describes the Swedes is 'family,'" Mark Prina said. "The Swedes are run by a small group of families, but every person that has ever been involved with the Swedes is considered a part of the Swedes' family."

Rodell
Gerdes

Paxton year-by-year leaders:

Batting

YEAR	TOP HITTER	AVG.
1968	Not available	NA
1969	John Hill	.317
1970	Jim Golden	.326
1971	Gordie Hull	.295
1972	Randy Peterson	.389
1973	Pat Prina	.406
1974	John Ireland	.345
1975	Bill Snyder	.269
1976	Pat Prina	.377
1977	Bill Snyder	.300
1978	Bobby Larson	.309
1979	Not available	n/a
1980	Bobby Larson	.385
1981	Don Manzke	.317
1982	Dennis Warford	.313
1983	Pat Herbert	.345
1984	Rod Hari	.437
1985	Kevin Johnson	.435
1986	Kevin Johnson	.319
1987	Kevin Dallas	.373
1988	Kevin Dallas	.413
1989	Jeff Rutledge	.319
1990	Not in league	NA
1991	Not in league	NA
1992	Chris Sorensen	.333
1993	Brad Cosgrove	.388
1994	Chris Sorensen	.419
1995	Chris Sorensen	.471
1996	Brad Cosgrove	.397
1997	Brad Cosgrove	.472
1998	Corey Fox	.453
1999	Ryan Dunsworth	.403
2000	Corey Fox	.393
2001	Trevor Fredrickson	.385
2002	John Grana	n/a
2003	Bryan Kurt	.444
2004	Corey Fox	.400
2005	Corey Fox	.372
2006	Luke Humphrey	.407
2007	Luke Humphrey	.462
2008	Luke Humphrey	.443
2009	Josh Federico	.378

NOTE: Leaders based on a minimum of 25 at-bats for a season

Pitching

YEAR	PLAYER	RECORD
1968	Dale Buzzard	1-8
1969	Rodell Gerdes	2-3
1970	Rodell Gerdes	5-4
1971	Randy Sorensen	2-2
1971	Jim Stamm	2-2
1972	Rodell Gerdes	10-2
1973	Vic Johnson	6-1
1974	Bill Snyder	7-3
1975	Dave Dettmering	5-1
1976	Bill Snyder	5-5
1977	Rick Johnson	5-3
1978	Rick Johnson	3-2
1979	Not available	n/a
1980	Randy Farney	3-3
1981	Not available	n/a
1982	Jeff Hedge	5-6
1983	Jeff Hedge	7-7
1984	Jeff Hedge	3-5
1985	Jeff Hedge	3-8
1986	Mike Walling	5-7
1987	Mike Walling	5-7
1988	Mike Walling	9-2
1989	Darrin Kregel	3-5
1990	Not in league	n/a
1991	Not in league	n/a
1992	Todd Grieff	3-6
1993	Ken Mutchmore	5-5
1994	Ken Mutchmore	6-4
1995	Ken Mutchmore	4-4
1996	Jamie Sailors	4-1
1997	Jamie Sailors	5-3
1998	Bob Tolone	7-2
1999	Aaron Taylor	7-2
2000	Aaron Taylor	7-2
2001	Andy Gerdes	7-5
2002	Andy Gerdes	11-0
2003	J.T. Furnish	5-0
2004	J.T. Furnish	7-1
2005	Scott Lucht	5-1
2006	Dylan Ward	6-1
2007	Dylan Ward	5-0
2008	Tyler Kilburn	5-2
2009	Grant Meyer	5-1

Paxton infielder Corey Fox

Thirty five years after the Paxton organization was formed, 10 persons stand out as the most influential in that time.

Alphabetically, they are:

Mark Coplea
Brad Cosgrove
Corey Fox
Jim Fox
Carl Hudson Jr.
Scott Lucht
Kenny Mutchmore
Mark Prina
Pat Prina
Jason Ronna

Paxton third baseman Mark Prina

Catching Up

The 2000s

2000

Nate Henrichs had four hits and Travis Brown had three for Buckley, which collected 16 hits and played errorless defense en route to a 14-3 title-game win against the Swedes in Paxton. Justin Schroeder (4-1) pitched eight innings and earned the win. Henrichs and Jake Krause hit homers for Buckley, whose coaches were Ken Johnson and Mark Scheiwe. Henrichs drove in six runs. Chad Rock had two hits for Paxton.

For the first time in 27 years, a Gifford-Flatville player won the batting title. Jeremy Hunt had a league-leading .439 average.

2001

For the second consecutive year, Justin Schroeder (8-1) pitched the Dutch Masters to the tourney title. Buckley won the game 6-3 despite being outhit 11-3 in Buckley by Gifford-Flatville.

Buckley, Gifford-Flatville, Paxton and Thomasboro were the league's only entries, the fewest number in the E.I.'s storied history. For T'boro — the powerhouse of the 1980s — this was its final year of membership.

By the end of the decade, however, interest would double and eight teams would be competing.

Buckley pitcher Justin Schroeder

Buckley had 17 players who appeared in at least five games: Travis Brown, Brian Daly, Joel Dodson, Trent Eshleman, Pat Hake, Chris Hawkins, Nate Henrichs, Jake Krause, Kurt Krumwiede, Micah Luebchow, Brian Naese, Brent Niebuhr, Josh Olsen, T.J. Posey, Todd Post, Mark Scheiwe, Justin Schroeder, Nate Whitney and Jason Wollard.

Gifford-Flatville outfielder Jeremy Hunt

2002

In a one-year experiment, the E.I. joined forces with the Bloomington-based Central Illinois Baseball League to produce a 12-team league. Two of the top three finishers were E.I. members. Paxton (19-2) won league honors while Buckley (15-5) shared the runner-up position with El Paso.

Buckley established its presence early, shutting out Bloomington 7-0 and 10-0 in the May 19, season-opening series. El Paso had both the highest scoring game and the best run production in a doubleheader, sweeping Olympia 22-11 and 14-12 on June 9. Paxton's regular season losses were to Lexington 8-7 in Week 1 and to Buckley 13-7 in Week 5.

At season's end, two tournaments were held. The top eight teams played at

Illinois Wesleyan University, in Bloomington, on Aug. 3-4. Third-seeded El Paso opened by beating sixth-seeded Gifford-Flatville in the quarterfinals and then upended No. 2 Buckley in the semifinals 8-3 and top-seeded Paxton in a 17-14 shootout in the finals.

A week later, at Paxton, four current or future E.I. teams played their own tournament. This time, fate smiled on the Swedes. They blanked Lexington in the semifinals 15-0 while Gifford-Flatville beat Buckley 13-12. In the Aug. 11 wrap-up, Paxton topped the Giflats 8-4 for first place and Buckley handed Lexington an 11-4 loss in the third-place game.

2003

The E.I. ended its association with the CIBL and expanded north and south to create a five-team league. Charleston and Clifton joined holdovers Buckley, Gifford-Flatville and Paxton.

In the tournament, Paxton captured the second of its three postseason titles in a row, edging Buckley 2-1. Andy Elson's sixth-inning single drove in Geoff Desmond, who had doubled, and broke a 1-1 tie. The Swedes' first run was courtesy of a hit by Chris Hughes.

Brian Naese's fourth-inning hit tied the game 1-1 for Buckley.

Thirteen players appeared in at least five games for the Swedes during the summer: Justin Chase, Andy Elson, Corey Fox, Joey Frerichs, J.T. Furnish, Kurtis Galyen, John Grana, Elliott Harriss, Chris Hughes, Bryan Kurt, Scott Lucht, Steve Pierce and Mark Prina.

2004

The major change was the manner of determining the postseason tournament champion. The single-elimination tournament, in effect for more than a quarter of a century, was transformed into a best-of-three format for the championship round.

In 2004 — as well as in 2005 — the team that won the opening game in the championship series was unable to secure the crown. Paxton rallied from a one-game deficit to upend Buckley in 2004. A year later, when the same teams met, Buckley showed its comeback abilities by overcoming a first-game loss to sweep the Swedes in the second-day doubleheader.

The championship series is set up with one Saturday game at the site of the lowest seeded survivor with the Sunday conclusion shifting to the top-seeded site for a possible doubleheader. The seedings for the tourney are based on finishes in the regular season.

Paxton was the ultimate survivor on the final day of the 2004 tournament. Trailing 1-0 in the series, the Swedes fell behind Buckley 5-0 in the third inning of the first Sunday game at home. The team rallied for a 7-6 victory thanks to a sacrifice fly by Andy Elson in the bottom of the ninth that drove in Wes Pabst.

The second-game comeback was even more improbable. Buckley held a 7-6 lead in the bottom of the 10th with two outs and an 0-2 count on the Swedes' Mark Prina. He reached base, and the momentum shifted back to the home team. Paxton scored the tying run when Buddy Dubois was hit by a pitch with the bases loaded. The next batter, Pabst, coaxed a walk to force in the decisive run in the Swedes' 8-7 stunner.

For the day, Paxton's Kurtis Galyen was 5 for 8. In the opener, he hit a single, double and triple. Buckley's Justin Schroeder finished his stint with a 14-strike-out performance.

Paxton faithful refer to the two games played on Sunday, Aug. 15 as the team's two most memorable contests.

2005

Mother Nature helped Buckley overcome a one-game deficit to capture the best-of-three title-game series from Paxton.

In the tournament opener, Luke Humphrey scored a run (on Andy Elson's sacrifice fly) and drove in a run as Paxton won 2-0. J.T. Furnish earned the win with Scott Lucht picking up his league-high seventh save.

Buckley ace Justin Schroeder (11-1) suffered his first loss. When the Sunday games were rained out the next day, Schroeder was able to take the mound a week later (Aug. 21) and fired a complete-game shutout as the Dutch Masters were triumphant 6-0.

In the decisive game, Alex Dye (5-2) pitched into the ninth as Buckley salvaged the championship with a 7-4 win. Dye pitched shutout ball until the fifth inning. Schroeder finished the game.

In the three games of the title series, Buckley played errorless defense.

The team's starters in the final game:

Catcher, Nick Runyon
First base, Scott Carley
Second base, Thomas Sullivan
Shortstop, Blake Schoonover
Third base, T.J. Posey
Left field, Ryne Scheiwe
Center field, Brandon McFarland
Right field, Ryan Morefield
Designated hitter, Rob Wicks
Pitcher, Alex Dye

The coaches were Ken Johnson, Gary Kingery, Brent Niebuhr and Mark Scheiwe.

2006

The E.I. swept an All-Star doubleheader from the Central Illinois Baseball League (CIBL) on Sept. 2 in Buckley. Dylan Ward struck out six batters in three innings in the first game, a 9-1 E.I. victory. Jeff Alexander and Kevin Wyman were each 3 for 4.

In the nightcap, Scott Lucht was the winner in a 4-2 game. The E.I. scored twice in the top of the seventh thanks to run-scoring hits by Joel Gher and Will Clark.

Paxton, which won tournament laurels, had 17 squad members who played in at least five games during the year: Andy Elson, Corey Fox, Chad Geiken, Andy Gerdes, Chris Hughes, Luke Humphrey, Aaron Ifft, Logan Johnson, Josh Landon, Scott Lucht, Greg Munz, Steve Pierce, Jerry Prina, Mark Prina, John

Smiley, Nick Swing and Dylan Ward.

2007

Playing at home in the tourney finals, Paxton pitchers Dylan Ward and Grant Meyer were the catalysts in a final-day sweep of Clinton. Ward pitched the distance in the opener, a 10-2 victory for the Swedes.

Meyer hurled five scoreless innings in the nightcap, a 7-1 Paxton triumph. The second game was called after $7 \frac{1}{2}$ innings when Clinton ran short of players. Chris Walters was ejected and Jack Mikel was injured, leaving the Zugs with eight healthy players.

2008

Brandon Duffy's complete game helped Lexington wrap up the tournament title with a 7-3 win against the Dutch Masters in Buckley. In the opening game of the series, Lexington prevailed 3-2 when Brett Moore's infield hit in the bottom of the seventh knocked in the run that snapped a 2-2 deadlock.

Twenty-three Lexington squad members played in at least six regular season games: Aaron Altman, Luke Baughman, Sean Berry, Blake Bloodworth, Kyle Cherney, Jordan Comadena, Brandon Duffy, Tony Eckhart, Mark Evans, Bruce Freed, Bob Huppert, Rob Inzinga, Chase Lowery, Casey McIntosh, Nick Meredeth, Brett Moore, Tim Newbury, Christopher Newsome, Skyler Peak, Mike Reu, Collin Salzenstein, Tanner Springer and Trevor Whately.

2009

Lexington won the tournament championship with a record-setting 25-2 verdict against Paxton in the title game. Thirteen players played in at least six regular season games for Lexington: J.D. Doll, Bob Huppert, Bo Kinder, Pat Kirchhofer, Luke Krippel, Craig Lutes, Shawn McGuire, Casey McIntosh, Jack Mikel, Brett Moore, Skyler Peak, Collin Salzenstein, E.J. Schiller and Trevor Whately. Jeff Doll

Lexington celebrates following a 2009 E.I. tournament triumph.

and Billy DuBois were the team's coaches.

For the first time in 13 years, the Eastern Illinois Baseball League's batting champion compiled a .500 average. Urbana native Tristan Facer, a first baseman for Gifford-Flatville, hit .500 with 16 hits in 32 at-bats. Facer was not available when the Giflats opened tournament play. Late in the summer, he signed a professional contract — as a pitcher — with an independent team from Gary, Ind., in the Northwest League.

The league's last .500 hitter was Buckley's Tom Waldrop, whose .563 average in 1996 set the E.I.'s single-season record.

Coaches 2009 E.I. All-Star First Team

Player	Team	Pos.
Jamison Miller	Effingham	P
Tyler Ware	Buckley	P
Jack Mikel	Lexington	C
Tristan Facer	Gifford-Flatville	Inf.
Josh Federico	Paxton	Inf.
Anthony Hecht	Effingham	Inf.
Kyle Suprenant	Buckley	Inf.
Kevin Bird	Royal	OF
Bo Kinder	Lexington	OF
Bryce Redeker	Buckley	OF
Seth Woods	Watseka	Utl.

Top players for the first decade of the 2000s, as chosen by league coaches:

Most outstanding player:

YEAR	PLAYER	TEAM
2000	Nate Linder	Paxton
2001	Jake Krause	Buckley
2002	John Grana	Paxton
2003	Bryan Kurt	Paxton
2004	Blake Schoonover	Buckley
2005	Nick Runyon	Buckley
2006	Luke Humphrey	Paxton
2007	Kevin Bird	Royal
2008	Luke Humphrey	Paxton
2009	Bo Kinder	Lexington

Most outstanding pitcher:

YEAR	PLAYER	TEAM
2000	Aaron Taylor	Paxton
2001	Justin Schroeder	Buckley
2002	Andy Gerdes	Paxton
2003	J.T. Furnish	Paxton
2004	Scott Lucht	Paxton
2005	Justin Schroeder	Buckley
2006	Paul Phillips	Buckley
2007	Justin Schroeder	Buckley
2008	Rob Inzinga	Lexington
2009	Tyler Ware	Buckley

2009 title-game recap

(as appeared in *The News-Gazette*)

LEXINGTON — Evan Fahrner spent part of nine years pursuing his dream; nine years pitching baseballs in the minor leagues.

The right-hander from Peoria, who was the winning pitcher in the 2005 Class AA Texas League All-Star Game, advanced as high as AAA. Since his release in 2007, Fahrner's passion for the game has not waned.

He was the starter — and the winner — as Lexington defended its Eastern Illinois Baseball League tournament crown with a record-setting 25-2 conquest of Paxton in the 2009 finale, a win that clinched the best-of-three series in two games.

Though he is now in the everyday working world — at State Farm — Fahrner said it's not a comedown to pitch in an amateur league.

"It's not difficult at all," said Fahrner, who made 290 career minor league appearances. "It keeps you in the game. It's fun."

After he reached his predetermined (by manager Billy DuBois) limit of five innings, left-hander Michael Kellar followed Fahrner to the mound.

Kellar, a former Ridgeview athlete, can relate to Fahrner's quest. He spent Saturday at a tryout in Peoria with Cubs' minor league roving pitching coach Mark Riggins.

"It didn't go as well as I'd have liked," Kellar said.

Sunday's outing did. Kellar retired all six batters he faced, ending both the sixth and seventh innings with strikeouts.

His stint helped boost his confidence for a tryout he'll have in five days with the Atlanta Braves' organization.

"It was nice to throw and do good for a couple of innings," Kellar said.

Paxton scored in the top of the first inning with Mark Prina driving in Jake Jurczak for a 1-0 Swedes' lead. Lexington, however, answered by scoring at least three runs in six of the first seven innings.

League MVP Bo Kinder, from Clinton, led the 21-hit assault by hammering three extra-base hits — including a grand slam — and driving in seven runs.

"I've known Coach (Pat) Prina for a while and I know his mentality. They'll scrap and keep going," Kinder said. "When you can get a run against them, you take it."

Teammate Trevor Whately, from Prairie Central, went 4 for 5, including a three-run homer.

The difference in the league's two finalists was not what was represented on the scoreboard, according to DuBois.

"On Saturday, nine of my starters had played college ball this year and today, seven had," Dubois said. "That was 50-60 games before you get to summer, and we played more than 40 (finishing 34-7).

"I have five guys who had over 120 at-bats this summer. They've faced all kinds of pitching."

Kellar enjoyed the opportunity.

"For as many games as we played, it was almost like a summer collegiate season," he said.

Mark Prina, one of Paxton's coaches, understands the advantage. Earlier this decade, the Swedes were scheduling midweek games to help college-age players stay sharp.

"Six or seven years ago, we were doing that and the number of pitchers you need to do that makes you deeper on Sundays," he said. "No question, that's a benefit when you have enough guys who want to do that."

Lexington broke the championship-game record for runs scored (19 by Gifford-Flatville in 1990) and for winning margin (14 runs by Rantoul in 1971). In the championship series, there is no 10-run rule.

The repeat title provided vindication for DuBois.

"When I tried to get in the league (after the 2006 season), I called four people, two laughed at me and said we couldn't compete and two said come on in," DuBois said.

"We've been known for good pitching. This year, we had good pitching and good hitting."

Besides Whately and Kinder, Jack Mikel and Jeff Doll each whacked four hits in the title game. Corey Fox had two of Paxton's four hits.

"It was a success for us to get to this point," Mark Prina said. "To be in the championship game will be huge in the future.

"We have the veterans and as we move to the twilight of our career, we have to find the youth to be our catalyst."

Paxton closes with a 13-11 record.

The tourney trail

In the first six years the Eastern Illinois Baseball League tournament champion has been determined by a best-of-three series instead of one title game, it has only been an advantage to win Game 1 half the time. A look at the results:

YEAR	OUTCOME
2009	Lexington swept Paxton in two games
2008	Lexington swept Buckley in two games
2007	Clinton won the opener before Paxton won the next two games
2006	Paxton swept Buckley in two games
2005	Paxton won the opener before Buckley won the next two games
2004	Buckley won the opener before Paxton won the next two games

Champions

The breakdown on all-time tourney titlists, which includes the three years (1933-35) before the league was "officially" known as the E.I. League:

E.I. tournament championships

TEAM	TITLES
Buckley	12
Gifford-Flatville	12
Royal	11
Thomasboro	9
Flatville	5
Paxton	5
Champaign Knights	3
Champaign Plumbers	3
Charleston-Mattoon	2
Lexington	2
Mattoon	2
Monticello	2
Rantoul	2
Seymour	2
Champaign Dexters	1
Champaign Eagles	1
Chanute AFB	1
Ivesdale	1
Urbana Merchants	1

Regular-season titles (since 1936)

TEAM	TITLES
Buckley	18
Gifford-Flatville	11
Royal	11
Thomasboro	8
Rantoul	7
Paxton	6
Champaign Eagles	4
Flatville	4
Mattoon Warriors	4
Seymour	4
Champaign Plumbers	3
Champaign Dexters	2
Danville	2
Tolono	2
Campus Legion	1
Champaign Colts	1
Champaign Knights	1
Chanute AFB	1
Effingham	1
Loda	1
Monticello	1
Sidney	1

NOTE: Titles listed include outright and shared championships as well as division pennants for the years there were two divisions.

Lexington Snipes

The Lexington team was created during the winter of 2000, with the process starting at a little bar in the village, Kemp's Upper Tap.

Billy DuBois and some of his high school buddies were reminiscing about when they helped their high school win the Class A state championship a decade earlier with a 25-3 record in the spring of 1990 when Eddie Moore was the head coach.

The conversation alternated between who was the team's best player to whether they could still play competitively as they approached their 30th birthdays.

DuBois had played for Paxton's E.I. team during the summers while he was in college and the league left a lasting impression.

"I recall the big crowds and the tough competition," he said.

He soon found he wasn't alone in wanting to play baseball.

"I started making a few phone calls to some of my old buddies," DuBois said. "All of them expressed interest in getting a team together and playing again."

In 2001, the Snipes joined Bloomington, Farmer City, El Paso, Normal, Olympia and Prairie Central in the Central Illinois Baseball League.

"The average age was 26 years old," DuBois said.

The Lexington team was 10-10 in its league games and 12-14 overall.

The following summer, the CIBL and the E.I. leagues merged for a one-season experiment.

"The competition was much harder," said DuBois, whose team was 4-16 in league play and 8-24 overall in 2002.

It was an eye-opening venture.

"I realized how tough the E.I. League was and that maybe the 1990 Class A state champions just can't compete with the kids these days," DuBois said.

By the time the 2003 summer season started, the CIBL and E.I. were back to being separate leagues. DuBois started adding collegiate players to his roster and the Snipes fared well in the Bloomington-area CIBL.

In 2006, Lexington won the CIBL championship.

"I realized this league was fun, but not as competitive as I wanted and I was looking to make a change," said DuBois, whose role had shifted from playing to coaching.

He made contact with commissioners of the E.I. League and his squad was welcomed for the start of the 2007 season.

In the Snipes' inaugural season, they placed third in their division during the regular season and suffered a first-round tournament loss.

"That was not what I hoped," said DuBois, who had a busy — but productive — offseason.

"That winter, I called every college baseball player in the area and got a good response," he said.

A common theme, however, was that the college athletes were seeking to play more often than the Sunday-to-Sunday format that is a staple of the E.I.

Knowing that he had a strong roster of players, DuBois scheduled 20 non-league games.

"Adding more games was great for the players because they enjoy playing and it gave us more practice for the E.I. League tournament," DuBois said.

Lexington had a strong regular season run, finishing second in the North Division, and capped the 2008 season by winning the tournament title.

E.I. Pitcher of the Year Robert Inzinga was the staff ace. He compiled an 8-1 record to go with a 1.34 earned run average.

Suddenly, Dubois found it easier to fill his roster.

"I expected to have to work at recruiting players once again," he said, "but this time it was different. We had made a name for ourselves and I had several calls from players and their coaches regarding playing for the Snipes. I had interest in teams from all over the state."

With several newcomers joining a strong returning nucleus, Lexington matched its success from the previous summer, ending the regular season in second place and following with a tournament championship.

The Snipes' top two hitters, catcher Jack Mikel (.471 average) and outfielder Bo Kinder (.409), joined the team in 2009. Kinder earned E.I. Player of the Year honors.

The pitching staff featured eight hurlers with wins and a staff earned run average of 2.92. Right-hander Brandon Duffy (4-0 the year before) was 5-1, newcomer Pat Kirchhofer was 4-3 and former minor league Class AA All-Star Evan Fahrner was 3-0.

For all games played in 2009, the Snipes were 34-7.

"Looking back, the switch to the E.I. League was the best move the Snipes could have made," DuBois said. "As far as I'm concerned, Sunday ball in the E.I. is as tough as it gets."

To be prepared for the weekly Sunday challenges, DuBois prepared an ambitious schedule. In the summer of 2009, Lexington played a national team (Team Lithuania), a state champion from an Iowa league and several NABF national qualifiers.

It's a pattern he hopes to follow in the future.

2010

That there remains interest in the league is clear. In February, the E.I. League made its debut on Facebook. Within 24 hours, 50 friends had signed on. Within two months, the total had surpassed 200.

The E.I. website (eibaseball.com), which was launched in 2007, had nearly 54,000 visitors by mid-May.

Here's hoping the next 75 years will be as grand and memorable as the first 75.

The roster of teams and managers for the 75th anniversary season:

    Buckley, Brent Niebuhr
    Gifford-Flatville, Erik Plotner
    Lexington, Jeff Doll

Paxton, Mark Prina
Royal, Michael Harper
Urbana, Jason Campbell
Watseka, Brian Brutlag
Commissioners:
Fred Kroner, President
Trent Eshleman, Secretary
Jeff Teske, Treasurer
Louie Krumwiede
Joe Lamb
Norlyn Loschen
Pat Prina

Hometown Proud

2009 Paxton Swedes

The perfect combination for creating a successful summer baseball team is to mix the experience of proven veterans with the exuberance of youngsters.

The blend is one Paxton's Swedes have used to become the most dominant Eastern Illinois Baseball League postseason team in the first decade of the 2000s. Paxton won five tournament titles in the decade.

Paxton pitcher Scott Lucht

The Swedes' 2009 lineup included athletes like Mark Prina, who had played in 212 consecutive E.I. games, Corey Fox, who made the 700-mile commute from Gaffney, S.C., where he is the Limestone College women's basketball coach, Scott Lucht and Andy Gerdes, both of whom have played at least 12 summers for the team.

"We have had the same core nucleus of players for the past 10 years, but the fact that we have been adding a few younger players over the years has contributed greatly to the success of our team," said Jason Ronna, who joined Mark Prina and his father, Pat Prina, as the game day coaches.

"We've been able to add pieces to the puzzle each year to continue to be successful," Mark Prina said.

Among the newcomers who made an impact in 2009 were recent high school graduates T.J. Lutz (Gibson City-Melvin-Sibley) and Jordan Scherf (Milford) as well as junior-to-be Dylan Overstreet (Paxton-Buckley-Loda).

"These guys, along with a few others, have helped remake the Swedes," Mark Prina said. "The young guys have grown up quickly and have been contributing throughout the second half of the year.

"It has given a boost to the veterans to see the hunger of the young guys."

Lutz was the winning pitcher in the 15-inning quarterfinal win against Gifford-Flatville. Scherf scored the winning run in the semifinal upset of top-seeded Buckley.

In both of its 2009 tournament wins, Paxton (13-11) trailed after seven innings.

What made the year's surge more unlikely was the loss of outfielder Luke Humphrey, the 2007 batting champion and the 2008 E.I. Most Valuable Player. He suffered a ligament injury in his elbow on June 14 and did not return to action.

"It has been a roller-coaster year," Mark Prina said. "At the beginning of the year, we thought we had put together one of our best teams ever."

131

Injuries, along with weekend job commitments, prevented the full lineup from being assembled the final half of the summer. The team, however, didn't discount its chances in the tournament.

"We have a group of guys who never give up and who love to compete," Mark Prina said. "I think we can continue competing for a long time as our younger players continue to develop."

Ronna said it's not surprising that Paxton has developed one of the most loyal fan followings on a weekly basis.

"The key factor is the number of local players," Ronna said. "The fact that a lot of these players are from Paxton, Cissna Park, Gibson City, Onarga or Rantoul (17 of 25) contributes to the good crowds and gives the players a sense of community pride. Playing for your local team kind of makes you want to compete at a higher level of intensity."

In the tournament championship game for the 10th time in the past 12 years, Paxton tried unsuccessfully to match a record held by Royal for the most tournament crowns in any eight-year period. Royal won six titles between 1967-74. The first tournament, held in 1933, predated the E.I. by three years.

Paxton's lineup for the 2009 tournament opener featured Gerdes (first base), Fox (second base), Josh Landon (shortstop), Mark Prina (third base), Jerry Prina (left field), Jake Jurczak (center field), Scherf (right field), Pete Hornstein (catcher) and Grant Meyer (pitcher).

Lucht, who pitched in 13 of the team's first 22 games, was available for relief duty. He worked 6 $^2/_3$ innings of scoreless relief in the semifinals against the Giflats and among squad members who have thrown at least 10 innings during the summer, Lucht had the best earned run average (2.33).

"He's one of the best relievers this league has ever seen," Mark Prina said.

Statistics and records

E.I. records

Following are the single-season batting and pitching records for regular season games, as known, for the 74-year existence of the Eastern Illinois Baseball League:

BATTING

CATEGORY	NAME, TEAM, YR.	RECORD
AB	Gerald Wilson, Mattoon, 1983	116
R	Andy Small, Thomasboro, 1992	37
H	Steve Darnell, Danville, 1986	44
RBI	Bill Elliott, Thomasboro, 1984	40
AVG.	Tom Waldrop, Buckley, 1996	.563
2B	Dave Gibson, Buckley, 1987	13
2B	John Patrizi, Tolono, 1988	13
3B	Ev Hall, Loda, 1949	6
3B	Russ Hyde, Champaign, 1950	6
3B	Larry Ruschel, Gifford, 1955	6
3B	John Sherman, Gifford, 1956	6
3B	Larry Hupp, Monticello, 1977	6
3B	Gerald Wilson, Mattoon, 1981	6
HR	Bill Elliott, Thomasaboro, 1983	13
BB	Dave Murray, Tolono, 1989	28
HBP	Ryan Dunsworth, Paxton, 1999	10
OB AVG.	Tom Waldrop, Buckley, 1996	.607
SLUG PCT.	Ken Crawford, Thomasboro, 1995	1.044
SB	Dave Rear, Gifford-Flatville, 1985	24
SB	Jerome Nelson, Tolono, 1989	24

Steve Darnell Dave Gibson John Patrizi Dave Rear Jerome Nelson

Catching Up

PITCHING

CATEGORY	NAME, TEAM, YR.	RECORD
ERA	Justin Schroeder, Buckley, 2005	0.83
IP	Ehm Franzen, Flatville, 1951	146
CG	Ed Logan, Rantoul, 1987	13
SO	Lee Schinker, Dexters, 1964	182
W	Art Goreham, Monticello, 1955	14
W	Loren Tate, Knights, 1958	14
BB	Justin Schroeder, Buckley, 2001	0.52

NOTE: Records are for regular season E.I. games only and do not include tournament play. A minimum of 50 innings pitched was required to be considered for ERA and walks per seven innings. Complete statistics were not available for some years.

E.I. batting champions

YEAR	NAME, TEAM	AB	R	H	AVG.
1936	Ed Knuepple, Buckley	82	31	36	.439
1937	Noel Pike, Champaign Plumbers	64	19	31	.484
1938	Harry Combes, Champaign Plumbers	64	24	29	.446
1939	Dill Seymour, Seymour	75	15	34	.453
1940	Julius 'Bud' Wiese, Tuscola	59	7	26	.441
1941	Walt Flanigan, Champaign Plumbers	na	na	na	.486
1942	Dill Seymour, Seymour	31	9	16	.516
1943	John Flessner, Flatville	42	11	16	.381
1944	Bryan Howell, Chanute AFB	na	na	na	.468
1945	Don Cribbett, Royal	52	16	23	.442
1946	Ed Wickland, Campus Legion	43	na	21	.489
1947	Carl Wolf, Buckley	52	20	28	.538
1948	Eldred 'Bumps' Hadley, Thomasboro	55	14	26	.473
1949	Bud Bitter, Sidney	79	24	37	.468
1950	Ev Hall, Loda	75	24	34	.453
1951	Bob Ems, Thomasboro	36	10	18	.500
1952	Bob Ems, Thomasboro	33	7	16	.485
1953	Elzer Marx, Flatville	41	10	18	.439
1954	Tony Johnson, Royal	38	8	18	.474
1955	Rocky Racklovits, Champaign Knights	42	14	21	.500
1956	Charlie Due, Champaign Knights	61	21	31	.508
1957	Frank Thomas, Villa Grove	41	9	21	.512
1958	Loren Tate, Champaign Knights	51	21	23	.489
1959	Cliff Adkinson, Champaign Eagles	52	16	26	.500
1959	Butch Kemmer, Loda	32	7	16	.500
1959	Norm Franzen, Gifford-Flatville	32	3	16	.500
1960	Gary Olden, Tuscola	36	7	17	.472
1961	Carl Cooke, Royal	42	13	21	.500
1962	Ernie Westfield, Champaign Eagles	36	n/a	16	.444

Year	Name, Team			
1963	Lou Ryniec, Royal	57	16	28	.491
1964	Roy Radmaker, Champaign Eagles	57	15	30	.526
1965	Guy Corey, Danville	57	11	24	.421
1966	Gordie Hull, Buckley	38	13	17	.447
1967	Louie Krumwiede, Buckley	44	10	20	.455
1968	Dale Metcalf, Rantoul	38	15	17	.447
1969	Bill Gillispie, Champaign Eagles	55	20	28	.509
1970	Willie Southall, Champaign Eagles	39	12	16	.410
1971	Bill Gillispie, Rantoul	62	14	31	.500
1972	Bill Gillispie, Rantoul	89	26	43	.436
1973	Ken Barenthin, Gifford-Flatville	58	20	29	.500
1974	Tom Posey, Buckley	54	18	27	.500
1975	Rich Connell, Royal	55	19	24	.436
1976	Tom Posey, Buckley	75	22	36	.480
1977	Howie Walker, Mahomet	72	23	34	.472
1978	Steve Maddock, Royal	76	23	33	.434
1979	Wade Bradley, Mattoon	77	33	35	.465
1980	Scott Lockhart, Buckley	67	16	30	.448
1981	Bobby Larson, Thomasboro	66	21	30	.455
1982	Bill Elliott, Thomasboro	84	27	38	.452
1983	Chris Slack, Monticello	93	26	40	.430
1984	Mike Johnson, Danville	75	23	39	.520
1985	Kevin Johnson, Paxton	85	25	37	.435
1986	Kenton Carley, Buckley	84	18	38	.452
1987	Joe Dunham, Thomasboro	71	16	33	.465
1988	Jeff Thompson, Danville	88	23	42	.477
1989	Jerome Nelson, Tolono	72	29	34	.472
1990	Tim Kemmer, Buckley	65	20	32	.492
1991	Mike Dokey, Tolono	70	19	33	.471
1992	Andy Small, Thomasboro	66	37	32	.485
1993	Ken Crawford, Thomasboro	56	24	27	.482
1994	Ken Crawford, Thomasboro	70	18	33	.471
1995	Ken Crawford, Thomasboro	68	27	37	.544
1996	Tom Waldrop, Buckley	55	19	31	.563
1997	Brad Cosgrove, Paxton	72	22	34	.472
1998	Justin Stone, Crawford County	45	16	21	.467
1999	Ryan Alexander, Tolono	45	16	21	.467
2000	Jeremy Hunt, Gifford-Flatville	41	13	18	.439
2001	Jake Krause, Buckley	61	14	26	.426
2002	Not available	n/a	n/a	n/a	n/a
2003	Bryan Kurt, Paxton	45	n/a	20	.444
2004	Blake Schoonover, Buckley	82	27	39	.476
2005	Joe Havis, Chambana	50	17	22	.440

2006	Brad Netzel, Clifton	79	13	37	.468
2007	Luke Humphrey, Paxton	52	17	24	.462
2008	Kevin Wyman, Buckley	47	18	23	.489
2009	Tristan Facer, Gifford-Flatville	32	7	16	.500

E.I. home run leaders

YEAR	NAME, TEAM	NO.
1945	Ed Paprocki, Illini Vets	2
1945	Tony Tangalos, Illini Vets	2
1946	Not available	n/a
1947	Len Hull, Buckley	3
1947	Ed Knuepple, Buckley	3
1948	Bud Bitter, Thomasboro	3
1948	Francis Gleason, Buckley	3
1948	Eldred 'Bumps' Hadley, Thomasboro	3
1948	Ed Knuepple, Buckley	3
1948	John Kopka, Seymour	3
1949	Bud Bitter, Sidney	6
1950	Vern Echols, Champaign	3
1950	Eldred 'Bumps' Hadley, Loda	3
1950	Virgil Scheiwe, Buckley	3
1951	Eldred 'Bumps' Hadley, Loda	6
1952	Bill Clark, Rantoul	2
1952	Bob Ems, Thomasboro	2
1952	W.R. Estep, Rantoul	2
1952	Lee Eilbracht, Flatville	2
1952	Don McAllister, Rantoul	2
1953	Jim Freeman, Champaign Knights	8
1954	Jim Freeman, Champaign Knights	5
1955	Dick 'Rocky' Raklovits, Cham. Knights	3
1955	Jim York, Monticello	3
1956	Dick 'Rocky' Raklovits, Cham. Knights	9
1957	Charlie Due, Champaign Knights	5
1958	Larry Ruschel, Gifford-Flatville	4
1959	Ken Fletcher, Royal	6
1960	Gene Murray, Tuscola	3
1961	Ron Franzen, Loda	3
1961	Jim Freeman Champaign Eagles	3
1961	Ron Pirtle, Champaign Eagles	3
1962	Rochell Broome, Champaign Eagles	5
1963	Rochell Broome, Champaign Eagles	4
1963	Lou Ryniec, Royal	4
1964	Lou Ryniec, Champaign Dexters	10

Bobby Larson

Chris
Slack

Mike
Dokey

1965	Ron Franzen, Gifford-Flatville	5
1966	Val Bush, Rantoul	4
1967	Gayle Franzen, Rantoul	3
1967	Louie Krumwiede, Buckley	3
1968	Art Goldstein, Champaign Eagles	5
1969	Pete Hittmeier, Tuscola	3
1969	Willie McCullum, Champaign Eagles	3
1970	Denny Shelato, Rantoul	4
1971	Bill Gillispie, Rantoul	4

| Ken Fletcher | Bill Elliott | Les Hoveln | Jeff Demith | Mark McElwain |

1972	Deon Flessner, Royal	7
1972	Bill Gillispie, Rantoul	7
1973	Mitch Osterbur, Royal	6
1974	Warren Cox, Gibson City	4
1974	Ken Fletcher, Royal	4
1975	Norlyn Loschen, Gifford-Flatville	4
1976	Tom Bernett, Farmer City-Mansfield	6
1976	Jim Goss, Gifford-Flatville	6
1977	Steve Maddock, Royal	7
1978	Mark Steppe, Mattoon	5
1979	Laney Maulden, Decatur	4
1979	Gary Sebens, Monticello	4
1980	Bill Elliott, Thomasboro	7
1981	Bill Elliott, Thomasboro	5
1981	Chris Wicks, Champaign	5
1982	Bill Elliott, Thomasboro	9
1983	Bill Elliott, Thomasboro	13
1984	Les Hoveln, Royal	7
1985	Bill Elliott, Thomasboro	8
1986	Bill Elliott, Thomasboro	7
1987	Jeff Demith, Thomasboro	7
1988	John Patrizi, Tolono	9
1989	Bill Elliott, Thomasboro	7
1989	Mark Scheiwe, Buckley	7
1990	Mark McElwain, Rantoul	7
1991	Bob Mutnansky, Gifford-Flatville	10
1992	Andy Small, Thomasboro	8

Catching Up

1993	Bill Elliott, Thomasboro	7
1994	Ken Crawford, Thomasboro	6
1995	Ken Crawford, Thomasboro	9
1996	Ken Crawford, Thomasboro	11
1997	Shane Ring, Charleston-Mattoon	9
1998	Nate Henrichs, Buckley	5
1998	Scott Scharlau, Thomasboro	5
1999	Ken Crawford, Thomasboro	8
2000	Ken Crawford, Thomasboro	4
2000	Nate Henrichs, Buckley	4
2001	Jake Krause, Buckley	5
2002	Not available	n/a
2003	Kurtis Galyen, Paxton	2
2003	Nate Henrichs, Buckley	2
2003	Justin Willis, Gifford-Flatville	2
2004	Kurtis Galyen, Paxton	5
2005	Luke Humphrey, Paxton	3
2005	Shawn Porento, Clifton	3
2006	Luke Humphrey, Paxton	5
2007	Luke Humphrey, Paxton	3
2008	Tristan Facer, Gifford-Flatville	3
2009	Kevin Bird, Royal	2
2009	Anthony Hecht, Effingham	2
2009	Bryce Redeker, Watseka	2
2009	Kevin Wyman, Buckley	2

NOTE: Home run leaders not available prior to 1945.

Pitching pacesetters

The best regular season pitching records since the E.I. was officially created in 1936:

YEAR	NAME, TEAM	RECORD
1955	Art Goreham, Monticello	14-1
1958	Loren Tate, Knights	14-1
1949	Ehm Franzen, Flatville	13-2
1951	Ehm Franzen, Flatville	13-1
1939	Wallie Kimberlin, Seymour	13-2
1957	Pablo Labrador, Eagles	12-0
1972	Dan Lathrop, Rantoul	12-3
1977	Jerry O'Neill, Royal	12-2
1976	Mike Scholz, Gifford-Flatville	12-0
1983	John Widdersheim, Gifford-Flatville	12-1

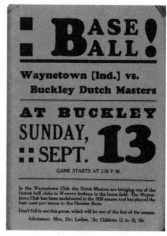

A poster advertising a 1936 baseball game in Buckley.

A poster advertising a 1938 baseball game in Buckley.

Home run leaders

The best regular-season home run totals since the E.I. was officially created in 1936:

YEAR	NAME, TEAM	HRs
1983	Bill Elliott, Thomasboro	13
1996	Ken Crawford, Thomasboro	11
1991	Bob Mutnansky, Gifford-Flatville	10
1964	Lou Ryniec, Champaign Dexters	10
1995	Ken Crawford, Thomasboro	9
1982	Bill Elliott, Thomasboro	9
1988	John Patrizi, Tolono	9
1956	Rocky Raklovits, Champaign Knights	9
1997	Shane Ring, Charleston-Mattoon	9

Batting leaders

The best regular season batting averages since the E.I. was officially created in 1936.

YEAR	NAME, TEAM	AVG.
1996	Tom Waldrop, Buckley	.563 (31 for 55)
1995	Ken Crawford, Thomasboro	.544 (37 for 68)
1947	Carl Wolf, Buckley	.538 (28 for 52)
1964	Roy Radmaker, Champaign Eagles	.526 (30 for 57)
1984	Mike Johnson, Danville	.520 (39 for 75)
1942	Dill Seymour, Seymour	.516 (16 for 31)
1957	Frank Thomas, Villa Grove	.512 (21 for 41)
1984	Lonnie West, Danville	.512 (21 for 41)
1996	Clint Benhoff, Crawford County	.511 (24 for 47)
1969	Bill Gillispie, Champaign Eagles	.509 (28 for 55)
1956	Charlie Due, Champaign Knights	.508 (31 for 61)

E.I. final yearly standings

1936 TEAM	W	L	PCT.	GB
Flatville	15	2	.882	—
Buckley	15	3	.833	1/2
Seymour	10	7	.588	5
Thomasboro	10	8	.556	5 1/2
Royal	9	9	.500	6 1/2
Leverett	7	9	.438	7 1/2
Chanute	6	11	.353	9
Sadorus	6	12	.333	9 1/2
Rankin	5	13	.278	10 1/2
106th Cavalry	4	13	.235	11

Tournament: 1st—Flatville

1937 TEAM	W	L	PCT.	GB
Champaign Plumbers	14	4	.778	—
Flatville	13	4	.765	1/2
Seymour	13	5	.722	1
Thomasboro	12	6	.667	2
Royal	11	7	.611	3
Buckley	8	8	.500	5
Sadorus	7	10	.412	6 1/2
Leverett	5	13	.278	9
Ivesdale	3	15	.167	11
106th Cavalry	2	16	.111	12

Tournament: 1st—Champaign Plumbers

1938 TEAM	W	L	PCT.	GB
Champaign Plumbers	13	5	.722	—
Thomasboro	12	6	.667	1
Seymour	11	6	.647	1 1/2
Flatville	10	7	.588	2 1/2
Buckley	8	8	.500	4
Royal	8	9	.471	4 1/2
Leverett	7	9	.438	5
Ivesdale	5	10	.333	6 1/2
Bellflower	5	11	.313	7
106th Cavalry	4	12	.250	8

Tournament (at Thomasboro):1st—Champaign Plumbers, 10 runs
2nd—Buckley, 9 runs
Other semifinalists: Royal, Thomasboro

1939 TEAM	W	L	PCT.	GB
Champaign Plumbers	15	3	.833	—
Seymour	15	3	.833	—
Tuscola	14	4	.778	1
Monticello	11	7	.611	4
Thomasboro	10	8	.556	5
Buckley	7	11	.389	8
Leverett	7	11	.389	8
Ivesdale	6	12	.333	9
Thawville	5	13	.278	10
106th Cavalry	0	18	.000	15

Tournament: 1st—Monticello

1940 TEAM	W	L	PCT.	GB
Buckley	13	5	.722	—
Champaign Plumbers	12	6	.667	1
Seymour	11	6	.647	1 1/2

Monticello	9	7	.563	3
Flatville	8	8	.500	4
Tuscola	8	10	.444	5
Thawville	7	11	.389	6
Thomasboro	7	11	.389	6
Leverett	6	11	.353	6 1/2
Ivesdale	6	12	.333	7

Tournament: 1st—Ivesdale, 8 runs
2nd—Thomasboro, 4 runs

1941 TEAM	W	L	PCT.	GB
Champaign Colts	10	2	.833	—
Champaign Plumbers	10	4	.714	1
Seymour	9	5	.643	2
Chanute	8	6	.571	3
Buckley	6	7	.462	4 1/2
Thomasboro	6	7	.462	4 1/2
Ivesdale	3	11	.214	8
Flatville	2	12	.143	10

Tournament: 1st—Champaign Plumbers

1942 TEAM	W	L	PCT.	GB
Royal	11	2	.846	—
Seymour	10	3	.769	1
Flatville	7	5	.583	3 1/2
Thomasboro	6	6	.500	4 1/2
Champaign	5	7	.417	5 1/2
Buckley	3	8	.273	7
Urbana	0	11	.000	10

Tournament: 1st—Seymour

1943 TEAM	W	L	PCT.	GB
Thomasboro	13	2	.867	—
Seymour	10	5	.667	3
Flatville	8	7	.533	5
Royal	8	7	.533	5
Buckley	6	9	.400	7
Ellis	0	15	.000	13

Tournament: 1st—Thomasboro

1944 TEAM	W	L	PCT.	GB
Chanute AFB	12	2	.857	—
Royal	11	3	.786	1
Seymour	8	6	.571	4
Thomasboro	8	6	.571	4
Navy	7	7	.500	5

Flatville	6	8	.429	6
Buckley	4	10	.286	8
Gifford	0	14	.000	12

Tournament: 1st—Chanute AFB

1945 TEAM	W	L	PCT.	GB
Royal	11	3	.786	—
Seymour	11	3	.786	—
Flatville	9	5	.643	2
Berghoff	8	6	.571	3
Illini Vets	8	6	.571	3
Buckley	7	7	.500	4
Sidney	1	12	.077	9 1/2
Champaign Colts	0	13	.000	10 1/2

Tournament: 1st—Royal

1946 TEAM	W	L	PCT.	GB
Seymour	13	3	.813	—
Buckley	14	4	.778	—
Royal	13	4	.765	1/2
Flatville	11	5	.688	2
Campus Legion	11	6	.647	3
Danville	10	8	.556	4
Gifford	5	10	.333	7 1/2
Champaign Colts	4	12	.250	9
Sidney	2	16	.111	12
Allerton	1	16	.059	12 1/2

Tournament (at Gifford): 1st—Flatville, 10 runs
2nd—Buckley, 2 runs
Other semifinalists: Royal, Seymour

1947 TEAM	W	L	PCT.	GB
Campus Legion	15	2	.882	—
Buckley	13	4	.765	2
Royal	12	5	.706	3
Flatville	12	6	.667	3 1/2
Seymour	9	7	.563	5 1/2
Champaign Colts	6	10	.375	8 1/2
Farm Bureau	5	12	.294	10
Gifford	5	12	.294	10
Thomasboro	4	13	.235	11
Sidney	4	14	.222	11 1/2

Tournament (at Flatville): 1st—Seymour, 16 runs
2nd—Buckley, 9 runs
Other semifinalists: Campus Legion, Royal

1948 TEAM	W	L	PCT.	GB
Seymour	11	3	.786	—
Buckley	10	4	.714	1
Flatville	9	5	.643	2
Thomasboro	9	5	.643	2
Royal	7	7	.500	4
Sidney	6	8	.429	5
Fisher	2	12	.143	9
Rantoul	2	12	.143	9

Tournament (at Royal): 1st—Royal, 13 runs
2nd—Seymour, 6 runs
Other semifinalists: Buckley, Thomasboro

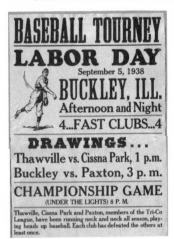

A poster advertising a 1949 baseball game in Buckley.

1949 TEAM	W	L	PCT.	GB
Flatville	15	3	.833	—
Sidney	15	3	.833	—
Royal	12	5	.706	2 1/2
Buckley	12	6	.667	3
Loda	12	6	.667	3
Champaign	8	9	.471	6 1/2
Rantoul	4	13	,235	10 1/2
Seymour	4	13	.235	10 1/2
Thomasboro	3	14	.176	11 1/2
Fisher	2	15	.118	12 1/2

Tournament (at Buckley): 1st—Royal, 6 runs
2nd—Flatville, 5 runs
Other semifinalists: Buckley, Loda

1950 TEAM	W	L	PCT.	GB
Loda	16	2	.889	—
Thomasboro	13	4	.765	2 1/2

Buckley	13	5	.722	3
Flatville	10	5	.667	4 ½
Champaign	11	7	.611	5
Royal	7	10	.412	8 ½
Ivesdale	6	11	.353	9 ½
Rantoul	5	12	.294	10 ½
Seymour	3	14	.176	12 ½
Sidney	1	15	.063	14

Tournament (at Buckley): 1st—Flatville, 12 runs
2nd—Loda, 5 runs
Other semifinalists: Buckley, Royal

A poster advertising the 1950 tournament finals in Buckley.

1951 TEAM	W	L	PCT.	GB
Flatville	13	1	.929	—
Buckley	10	4	.714	3
Loda	9	4	.692	3 ½
Champaign	6	7	.462	6 ½
Thomasboro	6	8	.429	7
Ivesdale	5	9	.357	8
Rantoul	5	9	.357	8
St. Joseph	1	13	.071	12

Tournament (at Buckley): 1st—Flatville, 15 runs
2nd—Rantoul, 3 runs
Other semifinalists: Buckley, Loda

1952 TEAM	W	L	PCT.	GB
Buckley	13	1	.929	—
Champaign	9	5	.643	4
Loda	9	5	.643	4
Flatville	9	6	.600	4 ½
Rantoul	7	7	.500	6

	W	L	PCT.	GB
Royal	5	9	.357	8
Ivesdale	2	11	.154	10 ½
Thomasboro	2	12	.143	11

Tournament (at Gifford): 1st—Buckley, 6 runs
2nd—Royal, 0 runs
Other semifinalists: Rantoul, Loda

1953 TEAM	W	L	PCT.	GB
Buckley	12	2	.857	—
Champaign Knights	12	2	.857	—
Royal	7	7	.500	5
Champaign Eagles	6	8	.429	6
Flatville	6	8	.429	6
Monticello	5	9	.357	7
Ivesdale	4	10	.286	8
Rantoul	4	10	.286	8

Tournament: 1st—Champaign Knights

Buckley's 1954 baseball team. In front, from left: Bill Weisenbarn, Skip Gharst, Bob Weisenbarn and Willard Krumwiede. In the middle row, from left: Max Lauderman, Lloyd Keever, Jerry Ditman, Virgil Scheiwe, Elmer Weber and Beryl Luecke. In back, from left: Mike Kaufmann, Dick Dannehl, Herb Kaufmann, Len Hull, Charlie Klann, Russ Plath and Tom Hull.

1954 TEAM	W	L	PCT.	GB
Flatville	12	2	857	—
Champaign Knights	10	4	.714	2
Buckley	8	5	.615	3 ½
Royal	7	6	.538	4 ½
Monticello	7	7	.500	5
Champaign Eagles	5	7	.417	5
Tolono	2	10	.167	9
Ivesdale	2	12	.143	10

Tournament: 1st—Flatville, 4 runs
2nd—Monticello, 3 runs

1955 TEAM	W	L	PCT.	GB
Monticello	15	3	.833	—
Champaign Knights	14	4	.778	1
Buckley	12	6	.667	3

Catching Up

Champaign Eagles	11	7	.611	4
Flatville	10	8	.556	5
Villa Grove	9	9	.500	6
Chanute	7	11	.389	8
Gifford	7	11	.389	8
Ivesdale	4	14	.222	11
Tolono	1	17	.056	14

Tournament (at Buckley): 1st—Monticello, 4 runs
2nd—Flatville, 1 run
Other semifinalists: Buckley, Chanute

1956 TEAM	W	L	PCT.	GB
Buckley	11	2	.846	—
Champaign Knights	11	3	.786	1/2
Flatville	9	5	.643	2 1/2
Newman	9	6	.600	3
Chanute	8	6	.571	3 1/2
Gifford	8	8	.500	4 1/2
Villa Grove	7	7	.500	4 1/2
Champaign Eagles	6	7	.462	5
Ivesdale	6	9	.400	6
Monticello	4	9	.308	7
Royal	4	10	.286	7 1/2
Champaign Colts	2	13	.133	10

Tournament (at Champaign Knights): 1st—Champaign Knights
2nd—Royal
Other semifinalists: Chanute and Gifford

1957 TEAM	W	L	PCT.	GB
Champaign Eagles	16	2	.889	—
Buckley	15	3	.833	1
Champaign Knights	13	5	.722	3
Gifford-Flatville	12	6	.667	4
Villa Grove	10	8	.556	6
Tuscola	7	9	.438	7
Ivesdale	7	11	.389	9
Royal	4	12	.250	11
Champaign Colts	3	15	.167	13
Newman	1	17	.056	15

Tournament: 1st—Gifford-Flatville, 7 runs
2nd—Champaign Knights, 4 runs

1958 TEAM	W	L	PCT.	GB
Buckley	14	2	.875	—
Gifford-Flatville	13	3	.813	1

Champaign Knights	12	3	.800	1 1/2
Champaign Eagles	11	5	.688	3
Villa Grove	10	6	.625	4
Loda	9	7	,563	5
Tuscola	7	8	.467	6 1/2
Champaign Colts	5	11	.313	9
Royal	5	11	.313	9
Fellers	4	12	.250	10
Sidney	4	12	.250	10
Ivesdale	1	15	.063	13

Tournament: 1st—Gifford-Flatville, 2 runs
2nd—Champaign Knights, 0 runs

1959 TEAM	W	L	PCT.	GB
Buckley	13	3	.813	—
Champaign Eagles	13	3	.813	—
Gifford-Flatville	13	3	.813	—
Royal	9	7	.563	4
Tuscola	9	7	.563	4
Champaign Knights	7	9	.438	6
Loda	7	9	.438	6
Villa Grove	7	9	.438	6
Gilman-Danforth	6	10	.375	7
Urbana	5	11	.313	8
Cissna Park	4	12	.250	9
Champaign Colts	3	13	.188	10

Tournament (at Gifford): 1st—Gifford-Flatville, 4 runs
2nd—Champaign Eagles, 3 runs
Other semifinalists: Buckley, Villa Grove

1960 TEAM	W	L	PCT.	GB
Buckley	12	4	.750	—
Champaign Eagles	12	4	.750	—
Royal	12	4	.750	—
Champaign Knights	10	6	.625	2
Loda	10	6	.625	2
Villa Grove	10	6	.625	2
Gifford-Flatville	9	6	.600	2 1/2
Tuscola	9	6	.600	2 1/2
Champaign Colts	6	10	.375	6
Urbana	3	13	.188	9
Cissna Park	2	14	.125	10
Seymour	0	16	.000	12

Tournament: 1st—Champaign Eagles

Catching Up

1961 TEAM	W	L	PCT.	GB
Royal	12	2	.857	—
Gifford-Flatville	11	3	.786	1
Champaign Eagles	10	4	.714	2
Buckley	9	5	.643	3
Champaign Knights	6	8	.429	6
Loda	4	10	.286	8
Cissna Park	2	12	.143	10
Villa Grove	2	12	.143	10

Tournament (at Royal): 1st—Royal, 5 runs
2nd—Gifford-Flatville, 1 run

1962 TEAM	W	L	PCT.	GB
Royal	11	3	.786	—
Champaign Knights	9	5	.643	2
Gifford-Flatville	8	6	.571	3
Champaign Eagles	7	6	.538	3 1/2
Buckley	6	6	.500	4
Champaign Dexters	6	6	.500	4
Chanute	4	10	.286	7
Cissna Park	1	10	.091	8 1/2

Tournament: 1st—Champaign Knights, 6 runs
2nd—Royal, 1 run

1963 TEAM	W	L	PCT.	GB
Champaign Dexters	11	2	.846	—
Champaign Knights	9	4	.692	2
Champaign Eagles	8	6	.571	3 1/2
Chanute	7	6	.538	4
Gifford-Flatville	7	7	.500	4 1/2
Buckley	6	8	.429	5 1/2
Royal	6	8	.429	5 1/2
St. Joseph	0	13	.000	11

Tournament (at Gifford): 1st—Royal, 6 runs
2nd—Champaign Dexters, 2 runs
3rd—Champaign Eagles, 7 runs
4th—St. Joseph, 5 runs

1964 TEAM	W	L	PCT.	GB
Champaign Dexters	11	4	.733	—
Champaign Eagles	9	6	.600	2
Gifford-Flatville	9	6	.600	2
Chanute	6	7	.462	4
Buckley	6	9	.400	5
St. Joseph	2	11	.154	8

Tournament (at Buckley): 1st—Champaign Dexters, 6 runs
2nd—St. Joseph, 2 runs
3rd—Gifford-Flatville, 7 runs
4th—Champaign Eagles, 2 runs

1965 TEAM	W	L	PCT.	GB
Danville	12	3	800	—
Gifford-Flatville	11	4	.733	1
Champaign Eagles	9	6	.600	3
Buckley	7	8	.467	5
Chanute	3	12	.200	9
St. Joseph	3	12	.200	9

Tournament: 1st—Buckley, 4 runs
2nd—Danville, 3 runs
3rd—Gifford-Flatville
4th—Champaign Eagles

Buckley's 1966 baseball team. In front, from left: Jim Varner, Wendell Harms, Jim Adams, Skip Gharst, Bill Weisenbarn, Joe Dwyer and Louie Krumwiede. In back from left: Rodell Gerdes, Jerry Niemann, Mick Larson, Rich Krumwiede, Rick Swearingen, Joe Grace, Dick Doran, Gordie Hull, Butch Kemmer, Don Varner and Lee Vedder.

1966 TEAM	W	L	PCT.	GB
Champaign Eagles	10	5	.667	—
Rantoul	10	5	.667	—
Buckley	8	7	.533	2
Gifford-Flatville	8	7	.533	2
St. Joseph	6	9	.400	4
Tuscola	3	12	.200	7

Tournament: 1st—Rantoul

1967 TEAM	W	L	PCT.	GB
Rantoul	12	3	.800	—
Buckley	8	6	.571	3 1/2
Champaign Merchants	8	7	.533	4
Royal	7	8	.467	5
Tuscola	5	10	.333	7
Champaign Eagles	4	10	.286	7 1/2

Tournament (at Buckley): 1st—Royal, 8 runs
2nd—Tuscola, 7 runs

Catching Up

3rd—Buckley, 12 runs
4th—Rantoul, 6 runs

1968 TEAM	W	L	PCT.	GB
Royal	11	2	.846	—
Rantoul	10	4	.714	1 1/2
Buckley	8	6	.571	3 1/2
Tuscola	8	6	.571	3 1/2
Champaign Eagles	3	11	.214	8 1/2
Paxton	1	12	.077	10

Tournament (at Royal): 1st—Royal, 7 runs
2nd—Buckley, 6 runs (10 innings)

1969 TEAM	W	L	PCT.	GB
Royal	11	3	.786	—
Rantoul	10	4	.714	1
Champaign Eagles	7	7	.500	4
Buckley	7	8	.467	4 1/2
Paxton	5	10	.333	6 1/2
Tuscola	3	11	.214	8

Tournament (at Royal): 1st—Royal, 1 run
2nd—Rantoul, 0 run
3rd–Champaign Eagles, 11 runs
4th—Tuscola, 5 runs

1970 TEAM	W	L	PCT.	GB
Royal	11	4	.733	—
Rantoul	10	5	.667	1
Buckley	7	8	.467	4
Champaign	6	9	.400	5
Paxton	6	9	.400	5
Gifford-Flatville	5	10	.333	6

Tournament (at Buckley): 1st—Royal, 7 runs
2nd—Rantoul, 0 runs

1971 TEAM	W	L	PCT.	GB
Rantoul	12	4	.750	—
Royal	10	6	.625	2
Gifford-Flatville	9	8	.529	3 1/2
Buckley	6	11	.313	6 1/2
Paxton	5	13	.278	8

Tournament (at Gifford): 1st—Rantoul, 15 runs
2nd—Royal, 1 run
3rd—Gifford-Flatville

1972 TEAM	W	L	PCT.	GB
Rantoul	21	9	.700	—
Paxton	20	10	.667	1
Buckley	19	11	.633	2
Royal	17	13	.567	4
Gifford-Flatville	11	19	.367	10
Thomasboro	2	28	.067	19

Tournament (at Royal): 1st—Royal, 10 runs
2nd—Paxton, 6 runs
Other semifinalists: Buckley, Rantoul

1973 TEAM	W	L	PCT.	GB
Gifford-Flatville	18	6	.750	—
Paxton	19	7	.731	—
Buckley	16	6	.727	1
Royal	17	10	.630	2 1/2
Rantoul	13	11	.542	5
Thomasboro	7	18	.280	11 1/2
Gibson City	6	20	.231	13
Tuscola	5	23	.179	15

Tournament (at Buckley): 1st—Royal, 11 runs
2nd—Buckley, 5 runs

1974	TEAM	W	L	PCT.	GB
Gifford-Flatville		16	4	.800	—
Rantoul		16	4	.800	—
Buckley		13	7	.650	3
Paxton		13	7	.650	3
Royal		8	10	.444	6
Tuscola		8	10	.444	6
Farmer City-Mansfield		6	14	.300	10
Gibson City		5	15	.250	11
Thomasboro		3	17	.150	13

Tournament (at Gifford): 1st—Gifford-Flatville, 1 run
2nd—Rantoul, 0 runs, (15 innings)
3rd—Buckley, 3 runs
4th—Paxton, 2 runs

1975 TEAM	W	L	PCT.	GB
Rantoul	17	3	.850	—
Royal	16	4	.800	1
Gifford-Flatville	15	5	.750	2
Paxton	14	6	.700	3
Mattoon	11	7	.611	5
Buckley	9	11	.450	8

	W	L	PCT.	GB
Champaign	7	11	.389	9
Thomasboro	5	15	.250	12
Monticello	4	14	.222	12
Tolono	4	14	.222	12
Farmer City-Mansfield	4	16	.200	13

Tournament (at Buckley): 1st—Gifford-Flatville, 9 runs
2nd—Buckley, 7 runs
3rd—Rantoul, 4 runs
4th—Paxton, 2 runs

1976 TEAM	**W**	**L**	**PCT.**	**GB**
Gifford-Flatville	20	3	.870	—
Buckley	17	6	.739	3
Thomasboro	17	6	.739	3
Rantoul	15	8	.652	5
Mattoon	12	11	.522	8
Royal	12	11	.522	8
Monticello	11	12	.478	9
Mahomet	10	13	.435	10
Paxton	10	13	.435	10
Farmer City-Mansfield	7	16	.304	13
Philo	7	16	.304	13
Tolono	0	23	.000	20

Tournament (at Gifford): 1st—Buckley, 9 runs
2nd—Gifford-Flatville, 5 runs
3rd—Thomasboro
4th—Rantoul

1977 North Division

TEAM	W	L	PCT.	GB
Royal	24	5	.828	—
Thomasboro	23	6	.793	1
Gifford-Flatville	17	9	.654	5 1/2
Buckley	16	12	.571	7 1/2
Paxton	14	14	.500	9 1/2
Rantoul	7	19	.269	15 1/2
Fisher	3	25	.107	20 1/2

1977 South Division

TEAM	W	L	PCT.	GB
Mattoon	20	7	.741	—
Monticello	17	10	.630	3
Mahomet	16	10	.615	3 1/2
Decatur	10	14	.417	8 1/2
Urbana-Champaign	10	16	.385	9 1/2

	W	L	PCT.	GB
Farmer City-Mansfield	6	20	.300	13 1/2
Tolono	5	21	.192	14 1/2

Tournament (at Royal): 1st—Mattoon, 8 runs
2nd—Royal, 6 runs
3rd—Gifford-Flatville
4th—Thomasboro

1978 North Division

TEAM	W	L	PCT.	GB
Gifford-Flatville	21	5	.808	—
Royal	22	6	.786	—
Buckley	20	8	.714	2
Thomasboro	15	11	.577	—
Rantoul	9	19	.321	13
Paxton	8	18	.308	13
Fisher	1	23	.042	19

1978 South Division

TEAM	W	L	PCT.	GB
Mattoon	22	6	.786	—
Mahomet	17	7	.708	3
Urbana-Champaign	18	10	.643	4
Monticello	14	12	.538	7
Farmer City-Mansfield	9	15	.375	11
Decatur	5	23	.179	17
Tolono	3	21	.125	17

Tournament (at Buckley): 1st—Gifford-Flatville, 2 runs
2nd—Mattoon, 0 runs

1979 North Division

TEAM	W	L	PCT.	GB
Gifford-Flatville	23	1	.958	—
Thomasboro	14	8	.636	8
Royal	15	9	.625	8
Rantoul	12	10	.545	10
Buckley	11	13	.458	12
Paxton	5	19	.208	18
Fisher	2	22	.083	21

1979 South Division

TEAM	W	L	PCT.	GB
Mattoon	21	1	.955	—
Monticello	11	8	.579	8 1/2
Mahomet	12	10	.545	9
Farmer City-Mansfield	9	10	.474	10 1/2
Urbana-Champaign	11	13	.458	11

Catching Up

	W	L	PCT.	GB
Decatur	8	15	.348	13 1/2
Tolono	4	19	.174	17 1/2

Tournament (at Gifford): 1st—Gifford-Flatville, 6 runs
2nd—Mattoon, 5 runs
3rd—Mahomet
4th—Monticello

1980 North Division

TEAM	W	L	PCT.	GB
Gifford-Flatville	18	4	.818	—
Buckley	17	9	.654	3
Thomasboro	18	10	.643	3
Royal	16	12	.571	5
Paxton	6	20	.231	14
Fisher	4	20	.583	15

1980 South Division

TEAM	W	L	PCT.	GB
Mattoon Warriors	22	2	.917	—
Monticello	18	6	.750	4
Mattoon Braves	18	10	.643	6
Tolono	12	12	.500	10
Champaign Pias	12	16	.429	12
Decatur	4	22	.154	19
Farmer City-Mansfield	3	25	.107	21

Tournament (at Gifford): 1st—Gifford-Flatville, 6 runs
2nd—Buckley, 4 runs

1981 TEAM	W	L	PCT.	GB
Gifford-Flatville	17	5	.773	—
Buckley	16	6	.727	1
Mattoon Warriors	13	6	.684	2 1/2
Champaign	15	7	.682	2
Thomasboro	13	9	.591	4
Royal	11	11	.500	6
Monticello	10	11	.476	6 1/2
Kankakee	9	11	.450	7
Rantoul	9	11	.450	7
Tolono	8	12	.400	8
Mattoon Braves	6	16	.273	11
Paxton	0	22	.000	17

Tournament (at Champaign): 1st—Mattoon, 9 runs
2nd—Champaign, 7 runs (12 innings)
Other semifinalists: Buckley, Kankakee

1982 TEAM	W	L	PCT.	GB
Thomasboro	22	4	.846	—
Gifford-Flatville	16	8	.667	5
Buckley	17	9	.654	5
Champaign	17	9	.654	5
Royal	15	11	.577	7
Mattoon	12	14	.462	10
Tolono	11	14	.440	10 1/2
Danville	9	15	.375	12
Rantoul	6	15	.286	13 1/2
Monticello	7	19	.269	15
Paxton	6	20	.231	16

Tournament (at Gifford): 1st—Gifford-Flatville, 5 runs
2nd—Thomasboro, 0 runs
3rd—Champaign
4th—Buckley

1983 TEAM	W	L	PCT.	GB
Gifford-Flatville	25	7	.781	—
Thomasboro	25	7	.781	—
Danville	21	11	.656	4
Buckley	18	13	.581	6 1/2
Paxton	13	19	.406	12
Royal	12	18	.400	12
Mattoon	12	20	.375	13
Monticello	10	19	.345	13 1/2
Tolono	5	27	.156	20

Tournament (at Gifford): 1st—Thomasboro, 2 runs
2nd—Gifford-Flatville, 0 runs
3rd—Buckley
4th—Danville

1984 TEAM	W	L	PCT.	GB
Thomasboro	17	9	.654	1
Gifford-Flatville	17	11	.607	1
Buckley	15	12	.555	2 1/2
Royal	14	13	.519	3 1/2
Argenta	14	14	.500	4
Danville	13	13	.500	4
Tolono	12	15	.444	5 1/2
Paxton	11	16	.407	6 1/2
Mattoon	8	18	.308	9

Tournament (at Gifford): 1st—Gifford-Flatville, 11 runs
2nd—Buckley, 10 runs
3rd—Thomasboro

4th—Danville

1985 TEAM	W	L	PCT.	GB
Thomasboro	23	7	.767	—
Buckley	20	9	.690	2 1/2
Tolono	20	9	.690	2 1/2
Danville	16	12	.571	6
Gifford-Flatville	16	12	.571	6
Rantoul	12	17	.414	10 1/2
Royal	10	18	.357	12
Argenta	6	21	.222	15 1/2
Paxton	5	23	.179	16

Tournament (at Rantoul): 1st—Thomasboro, 10 runs
2nd—Buckley, 1 run
3rd—Gifford-Flatville
4th—Rantoul

1986 TEAM	W	L	PCT.	GB
Danville	17	11	.607	—
Thomasboro	17	11	.607	—
Tolono	17	11	.607	—
Gifford-Flatville	16	12	.571	1
Buckley	14	14	.500	3
Rantoul	14	14	.500	3
Royal	9	19	.321	8
Paxton	8	20	.286	9

Tournament (at Danville): 1st—Buckley, 8 runs
2nd—Danville, 3 runs
3rd—Royal
4th—Paxton

1987 TEAM	W	L	PCT.	GB
Rantoul	20	8	.714	—
Thomasboro	17	11	.607	3
Royal	16	12	.571	4
Buckley	15	13	.536	5
Gifford-Flatville	15	13	.536	5
Danville	10	18	.357	10
Paxton	10	18	.357	10
Tolono	9	19	.321	11

Tournament (at Rantoul): 1st—Thomasboro, 8 runs
2nd—Rantoul, 4 runs

1988 TEAM	W	L	PCT.	GB
Buckley	19	9	.679	—
Paxton	18	10	.643	1

Tolono	16	12	.571	3
Rantoul	14	14	.500	5
Gifford-Flatville	13	15	.464	6
Danville	12	16	.429	7
Royal	10	18	.357	9
Thomasboro	10	18	.357	9

Tournament (at Buckley): 1st—Buckley, 17 runs
2nd—Tolono, 4 runs
3rd—Rantoul
4th—Paxton

1989 TEAM	W	L	PCT.	GB
Tolono	20	4	.833	—
Buckley	16	8	.667	4
Gifford-Flatville	14	10	.583	6
Thomasboro	13	11	.542	7
Danville	10	14	.417	10
Paxton	7	17	.292	13
Rantoul	4	20	.167	16

Tournament (at Tolono): 1st—Gifford-Flatville, 7 runs
2nd—Tolono, 1 run
3rd—Thomasboro
4th—Rantoul

1990 TEAM	W	L	PCT.	GB
Buckley	17	7	.708	—
Gifford-Flatville	15	9	.625	2
Tolono	13	11	.542	4
Thomasboro	11	13	.458	6
Rantoul	4	20	.167	13

Tournament (at Gifford): 1st—Gifford-Flatville, 19 runs
2nd—Rantoul, 8 runs
3rd—Tolono
4th—Buckley

1991 TEAM	W	L	PCT.	GB
Gifford-Flatville	20	4	.833	—
Buckley	19	5	.792	1
Tolono	14	10	.583	6
Thomasboro	10	14	.417	10
Rantoul	6	18	.250	14
Philo	3	21	.125	17

Tournament: 1st—Buckley, 6 runs
2nd—Gifford-Flatville, 2 runs

1992 TEAM	W	L	PCT.	GB
Thomasboro	18	3	.857	—
Buckley	16	6	.727	2 1/2
Champaign-Urbana	15	7	.682	3 1/2
Gifford-Flatville	12	10	.545	6 1/2
Tolono	7	15	.350	11 1/2
Paxton	6	18	.250	13 1/2
Rantoul	3	18	.143	15

Tournament (at Rantoul): 1st—Thomasboro, 9 runs
2nd—Buckley, 1 run

1993 TEAM	W	L	PCT.	GB
Gifford-Flatville	19	3	.864	—
Rantoul	19	6	.760	1 1/2
Buckley	19	9	.679	3
Champaign-Urbana	11	10	.524	7 1/2
Charleston-Mattoon	11	15	.423	10
Paxton	11	15	.423	10
Tolono	6	22	.214	16
Rantoul	5	21	.192	16

Tournament (at Gifford): 1st—Thomasboro, 9 runs
2nd—Gifford-Flatville, 7 runs

1994 TEAM	W	L	PCT.	GB
Buckley	18	6	.750	—
Paxton	15	9	.625	3
Thomasboro	15	9	.625	3
Charleston-Mattoon	12	12	.500	6
Gifford-Flatville	12	12	.500	6
Rantoul	10	14	.417	8
Royal	2	22	.042	16

Tournament (at Rantoul): 1st—Charleston-Mattoon, 11 runs
2nd—Thomasboro, 7 runs

1995 TEAM	W	L	PCT.	GB
Buckley	17	7	.708	—
Thomasboro	16	8	.667	1
Paxton	13	11	.542	4
Gifford-Flatville	11	13	.458	6
Charleston-Mattoon	8	16	.333	9
Rantoul	8	16	.333	9

Tournament (at Buckley): 1st—Thomasboro, 7 runs
2nd—Buckley, 5 runs

Buckley's 1996 regular season champions. In front, from left: Kurt Krumwiede, Todd Post, Ryne Scheiwe, Ken Johnson, Chris Hawkins and Trent Eshleman. In the middle row, from left: Brian Naese, Jason Garrelts, Steve Ekhoff, Andy Cotner, Doug Davis and Pat Hake. In back, from left: Mark Scheiwe, Nate Henrichs, T.J. Posey, Tom Waldrop, Jake Krause and Jerry Farris.

1996 TEAM	W	L	PCT.	GB
Buckley	21	5	.808	—
Thomasboro	20	5	.800	$^1/_2$
Charleston-Mattoon	16	12	.571	6
Paxton	11	12	.478	8 $^1/_2$
Gifford-Flatville	10	12	.455	9
Crawford County	10	15	.400	10 $^1/_2$
Rantoul	5	14	.263	12 $^1/_2$
Tolono	2	20	.091	17

Tournament (at Rantoul): 1st—Charleston-Mattoon, 13 runs
2nd—Thomasboro, 5 runs

1997 TEAM	W	L	PCT.	GB
Buckley	23	4	.852	—
Thomasboro	19	8	.704	4
Gifford-Flatville	14	9	.609	7
Charleston-Mattoon	12	11	.522	9
Paxton	12	11	.522	9
Crawford County	7	16	.438	14
Tolono	7	18	.280	15
Rantoul	2	19	.095	18

Tournament (at Buckley): 1st—Buckley, 11 runs
2nd—Gifford-Flatville, 6 runs
Other semifinalists: Paxton, Thomasboro

1998 TEAM	W	L	PCT.	GB
Thomasboro	18	5	.783	—
Buckley	16	7	.696	2
Paxton	15	8	.652	3
Crawford County	13	8	.619	4
Danville	12	10	.545	5 $^1/_2$
Gifford-Flatville	11	14	.440	8
Tolono-Monticello	10	14	.417	8 $^1/_2$
Charleston-Mattoon	3	17	.150	13 $^1/_2$

Catching Up

Rantoul	1	16	.059	14

Tournament (at Rantoul): 1st—Thomasboro, 8 runs
2nd—Paxton, 7 runs

1999 TEAM	W	L	PCT	GB
Buckley	20	3	.870	—
Paxton	17	6	.739	3
Thomasboro	15	6	.714	4
Gifford-Flatville	13	12	.520	8
Tolono-Monticello	11	12	.478	9
Danville	2	18	.100	16 1/2
Rantoul	0	21	.000	19

Tournament (at Buckley): 1st—Buckley, 8 runs
2nd—Paxton, 7 runs

2000 TEAM	W	L	PCT	GB
Paxton	18	5	.783	—
Buckley	16	5	.762	1
Gifford-Flatville	10	11	.476	7
Thomasboro	8	14	.364	9
Tolono-Monticello	1	18	.053	15

Tournament (at Paxton): 1st—Buckley, 14 runs
2nd—Paxton, 3 runs

2001 TEAM	W	L	PCT	GB
Buckley	17	7	.708	—
Paxton	14	10	.583	3
Gifford-Flatville	10	14	.417	7
Thomasboro	7	17	.292	10

Tournament (at Buckley): 1st—Buckley, 6 runs
2nd—Gifford-Flatville, 3 runs

2002 TEAM	W	L	PCT	GB
Paxton	19	2	.905	—
Buckley	15	5	.750	3 1/2
El Paso	15	5	.750	3 1/2
Fisher	11	9	.550	7 1/2
Gifford-Flatville	11	10	.524	8
Olympia	11	10	.524	8
Bloomington	10	10	.500	8 1/2
Prairie Central	10	10	.500	8 1/2
Farmer City	9	12	.429	10
Monticello	5	15	.250	13 1/2
Lexington	4	16	.200	15 1/2
Normal	2	18	.100	16 1/2

Tournament (at Paxton): 1st—Paxton, 8 runs
2nd—Gifford-Flatville, 4 runs
3rd—Buckley, 11 runs
4th—Lexington, 4 runs

2003 TEAM	W	L	PCT	GB
Paxton	14	2	.875	—
Buckley	10	6	.625	4
Gifford-Flatville	7	8	.467	6 1/2
Charleston	7	9	.438	7
Clifton	1	14	.067	12 1/2

Tournament (at Paxton): 1st—Paxton, 2 runs
2nd—Buckley, 1 run
Other semifinalists: Charleston, Gifford-Flatville

2004 TEAM	W	L	PCT	GB
Paxton	17	3	.850	—
Buckley	13	7	650	4
Chambana	13	7	.650	4
Gifford-Flatville	9	11	.450	8
Charleston	8	12	.400	9
Clifton	0	20	.000	17

Tournament (at Paxton): 1st—Paxton, 8 runs
2nd—Buckley, 7 runs (10 innings)
Other semifinalists: Chambana, Gifford-Flatville
BEST OF THREE FINALS: Paxton wins, 2 games to 1

2005 TEAM	W	L	PCT	GB
Buckley	17	3	.850	—
Paxton	13	7	.650	4
Clifton	10	10	.500	7
Chambana	8	10	.444	8
Charleston	5	13	.278	11
Gifford-Flatville	5	15	.250	12

Tournament (at Buckley): 1st—Buckley, 7 runs
2nd—Paxton, 4 runs
Other semifinalists: Chambana, Clifton
BEST OF THREE FINALS: Buckley wins, 2 games to 1

2006 TEAM	W	L	PCT	GB
Paxton	22	4	.846	—
Buckley	21	5	.808	1
Royal	12	11	.522	8 1/2
Clifton	13	14	.481	9 1/2
Chambana	11	15	.423	11
Gifford-Flatville	10	14	.417	11

Catching Up

Danville	6	20	.231	16
Mattoon	5	17	.227	15

Tournament (at Paxton): 1st—Paxton, 6 runs
2nd—Buckley, 4 runs
Other semifinalists: Gifford-Flatville, Royal
BEST OF THREE FINALS: Paxton won, 2 games to 0.

2007 North Division

TEAM	W	L	PCT	GB
Paxton	17	3	.850	—
Buckley	13	7	.650	4
Lexington	10	10	.500	7
Clifton	1	17	.056	15

2007 South Division

TEAM	W	L	PCT	GB
Royal	15	5	.750	—
Chambana	10	8	.556	4
Clinton	7	9	.438	6
Gifford-Flatville	3	17	.150	12

Tournament: 1st—Paxton
2nd—Clinton
BEST OF THREE SERIES: Paxton won, 2 games to 1.

2008 North Division

TEAM	W	L	PCT	GB
Buckley	15	4	.789	—
Lexington	13	7	.650	2 1/2
Paxton	11	9	.550	4 1/2
Clifton	1	19	.050	14 1/2

2008 South Division

TEAM	W	L	PCT	GB
Royal	13	7	.650	—
Effingham	9	9	.500	3
Gifford-Flatville	9	10	.474	3 1/2
Chambana	6	12	.333	6

Tournament (at Buckley): 1st—Lexington, 7 runs
2nd—Buckley, 3 runs
BEST OF THREE SERIES: Lexington won, 2 games to 0.

2009 North Division

TEAM	W	L	PCT	GB
Buckley	16	4	.800	—
Lexington	15	5	.750	1
Paxton	11	9	.550	5
Watseka	3	17	.150	13

2009 South Division

TEAM	W	L	PCT	GB
Effingham	13	5	.722	—
Gifford-Flatville	9	9	.500	4
Royal	6	12	.333	7
Urbana	1	13	.071	10

Tournament (at Lexington): 1st—Lexington, 25 runs
2nd—Paxton, 2 runs
BEST OF THREE SERIES: Lexington won, 2 games to 0.

E.I. team leaders

Records by the decades

1930s

TEAM	RECORD	PCT.	YRS. COMPETED
Tuscola	14-3	82.4	1
Champaign Plumbers	42-12	77.8	3
Flatville	38-13	74.5	3
Seymour	49-21	70.0	4
Monticello	11-7	61.1	1
Thomasboro	44-28	61.1	4

1940s

TEAM	RECORD	PCT.	YRS. COMPETED
Campus Legion	26-8	76.5	2
Chanute AFB	20-8	71.4	2
Royal	85-36	70.2	8
Champaign Plumbers	22-10	68.8	2
Loda	12-6	66.7	1
Seymour	96-54	64.0	10

1950s

TEAM	RECORD	PCT.	YRS. COMPETED
Buckley	121-33	78.6	10
Gifford-Flatville	38-12	76.0	3
Champaign Knights	79-30	72.5	7
Flatville	69-35	66.3	7
Loda	50-27	64.9	5
Champaign Eagles	68-39	63.6	7

1960s

TEAM	RECORD	PCT.	YRS. COMPETED
Danville	12-3	80.0	1
Rantoul	42-16	72.4	4
Champaign Dexters	28-12	70.0	3
Royal	70-30	70.0	7

Catching Up

Gifford-Flatville	55-33	62.5	6
Champaign Knights	34-23	59.6	4

1970s

TEAM	RECORD	PCT.	YRS. COMPETED
Mattoon Warriors	86-32	72.9	5
Gifford-Flatville	155-70	68.9	10
Royal	152-77	66.4	10
Buckley	134-93	59.0	10
Rantoul	132-92	58.9	10
Mahomet	55-40	57.9	4

1980s

TEAM	RECORD	PCT.	YRS. COMPETED
Champaign	32-16	66.7	2
Thomasboro	175-97	64.3	10
Gifford-Flatville	167-97	63.3	10
Buckley	167-102	62.1	10
Mattoon Warriors	67-60	52.8	5
Danville	108-110	49.5	8

1990s

TEAM	RECORD	PCT.	YRS. COMPETED
Buckley	186-59	75.9	10
Thomasboro	161-77	67.6	10
Champaign-Urbana	26-17	60.5	2
Gifford-Flatville	137-98	58.3	10
Paxton	100-90	52.6	8
Crawford County	30-39	43.5	3

2000s

TEAM	RECORD	PCT.	YRS. COMPETED
El Paso	15-5	75.0	1
Buckley	153-53	74.3	10
Paxton	156-54	74.3	10
Effingham	22-14	61.1	2
Royal	46-35	56.8	4
Fisher	11-9	55.0	1

OVERALL (Minimum 8 years in league)

TEAM	RECORD	PCT.	YRS. COMPETED
Champaign Knights	113-53	68.1	11
Buckley	964-501	65.8	74
Flatville	202-118	63.1	21
Loda	76-49	60.8	8

Gifford-Flatville	635-427	59.8	49
Mattoon Warriors	160-109	59.5	11

CUMULATIVE RECORDS (ranked by winning percentages)

TEAM	RECORD	PCT.	YRS. COMPETED
Campus Legion	16-8	76.5	2
El Paso	15-5	75.0	1
Champaign Plumbers	64-22	74.4	5
Champaign Dexters	28-12	70.0	3
Champaign Knights	113-53	68.1	11
Buckley	964-501	65.8	74
Flatville	202-118	63.1	21
Effingham	22-14	61.1	2
Loda	76-49	60.8	8
Champaign-Urbana	26-17	60.5	2
Gifford-Flatville	635-429	59.7	49
Mattoon Warriors	158-109	59.2	11
Champaign Eagles	147-104	58.6	17
Seymour	148-105	58.5	16
Mahomet	55-40	57.9	4
Berghoff	8-6	57.1	1
Illini Vets	8-6	57.1	1
Thomasboro	558-430	56.5	45
Royal	544-430	55.9	50
Champaign	84-71	54.2	9
Champaign Merchants	8-7	53.3	1
Lexington	42-38	52.5	4
Olympia	11-10	52.4	1
Bloomington	10-10	50.0	1
Navy	7-7	50.0	1
Prairie Central	10-10	50.0	1
Urbana-Champaign	39-39	50.0	3
Paxton	460-467	49.6	40
Villa Grove	55-57	49.1	7
Monticello	158-168	48.5	16
Chambana	48-52	48.0	5
Mattoon Braves	24-26	48.0	2
Danville	150-169	47.0	13
Kankakee	9-11	45.0	1
Chanute AFB	60-74	44.8	9
Clinton	7-9	43.8	1
Crawford County	30-39	43.5	3
Champaign Pias	12-16	42.9	1

Catching Up

Farmer City	9-12	42.9	1
Charleston-Mattoon	62-83	42.8	6
Tuscola	86-116	42.6	12
Rantoul	324-447	42.0	37
Leverett	32-53	37.6	5
Gilman-Danforth	6-10	37.5	1
Sadorus	13-22	37.1	2
Charleston	20-34	37.0	3
Argenta	20-35	36.4	2
Tolono	198-356	35.7	23
Thawville	12-24	33.3	2
Tolono-Monticello	22-44	33.3	3
Bellflower	5-11	31.3	1
Gifford	25-55	31.3	5
Newman	10-23	30.3	2
Farm Bureau	5-12	29.4	1
Sidney	33-80	29.2	7
Champaign Colts	39-99	28.3	9
Rankin	5-13	27.8	1
Farmer City-Mansfield	44-116	27.5	7
Ivesdale	60-162	27.0	14
Decatur	27-74	26.7	4
Fellers	4-12	25.0	1
Gibson City	11-35	23.9	2
Clifton	26-92	22.0	6
Philo	10-37	21.3	2
St. Joseph	12-58	17.1	5
Fisher	25-126	16.6	7
Cissna Park	9-48	15.9	4
Urbana	9-48	15.8	4
Watseka	3-17	15.0	1
106th Cavalry	10-59	14.5	4
Normal	2-18	10.0	1
Allerton	1-16	5.9	1
Ellis	0-15	0.0	1

About the author

Fred Kroner first started covering E.I. League baseball in 1975 as a part-time sports writer for the *Champaign-Urbana Courier.* He took over the beat full time in 1982, a year after joining *The Champaign-Urbana News-Gazette.* For 14 years, he covered a weekly doubleheader, weather permitting.

This is Kroner's third book. His first, *Citizen Pain,* was about NBA player Brian Cardinal, who grew up in Tolono, Ill. The next book, *Are You Ready,* profiled the career of Jim Sheppard, the former voice of University of Illinois football and men's basketball for more than two decades as the public address announcer.

Kroner has been recognized by The National Sportswriters and Sportscasters Association as the Illinois Sportswriter of the Year and four times earned recognition as the Newsman of the Year by the Illinois Wrestling Coaches and Officials Association.

In 2009, Kroner was inducted into the Illinois Basketball Coaches Association Hall of Fame.

At *The News-Gazette,* he is the prep sports coordinator and oversees all high school coverage, including selection of All-Area and All-State teams. He will celebrate his 30th anniversary at the newspaper in March of 2011.

Kroner and his wife, Emily, live in Mahomet. Between them, they have four children: Devin Kroner (Elizabeth), Sal Belahi (Shea), Jamel Belahi and Malika Belahi.